Buried Treasure

About the author

Caleb Wall advises companies on ways to enhance their social and environmental performance through improved management and engagement with the public. In his work Caleb works with management, staff and external stakeholders to create solutions to difficult problems and to find win-win outcomes.

These experiences have shown that the private sector — working in partnership with governments, NGOs and local communities — can make a solid contribution to community development, while making an equally solid contribution to long-term profitability.

Implementing the principle of creating value for shareholders, as well as for society, has seen Caleb work with a diverse range of companies, including: gold mines in Siberia, small business start-ups in Mongolia, agricultural producers in Tajikistan, and multinational corporations — some of which are featured in *Buried Treasure*.

Caleb's background includes work with the UN in Uzbekistan, as a policy advisor to the UN Environment Programme, as well as with the New Zealand government in Pakistan, Uzbekistan, Tonga and Vanuatu. He holds a PhD in Development Sociology, a Master of Arts in International Development and a Bachelor's degree in Political Science and Feminist Studies. When not travelling for work, he lives in Umbria, Italy.

caleb@localis-consulting.com

Buried Treasure

Discovering and
Implementing the Value of
Corporate Social Responsibility

Caleb Wall

LONDON AND NEW YORK

First published 2008 by Greenleaf Publishing Limited

Published 2017 by Routledge
2 Park Square, Milton Park, Abingdon, Oxon OX14 4RN
711 Third Avenue, New York, NY 10017, USA

Routledge is an imprint of the Taylor & Francis Group, an informa business

Copyright © 2008 Taylor & Francis

Cover by LaliAbril.com.

British Library Cataloguing in Publication Data:
A catalogue record for this book is available from the British Library.

ISBN-13: 9781906093105 (pbk)

Contents

Figures, tables and boxes

Figures

Tables

Boxes

Foreword

Ola Ullsten

Chairman of the World Council for Corporate Governance
Former Prime Minister of Sweden

In this book Caleb Wall makes the case that business exists, primarily, to serve its owners. The obligation of managers is to maximise investor returns and the job of staff is to create wealth for the business. But in maximising returns, says the author, it is crucial to look beyond the next quarterly result, further into the future, and that is, he argues, where ethics and a corporation's social responsibilities come in. This is where acknowledging a firm's obligations, primarily to the shareholders but also to stakeholders, staff and the environment, is a powerful tool in driving improved social, environmental and ultimately financial performance.

The author categorises corporations into three groups according to their approach to social and environmental matters. These are ranked as irresponsible corporations, who do not care much about either societal goals or their own social image. Next along the continuum are compliant corporations, those that abide by the laws but play no role in improving them or in enhancing their social and environmental impact. Finally there are proactive corporations, which provide leadership and help to realise the competitive power of ethical behaviour. These firms acknowledge their social and environmental impacts — they then find ways to seize on the opportunity to make environmental protection and other social goals a part of their business strategy.

Climate change can be a useful example when it comes to corporate ethics and social responsibilities. We all have to do our part as individuals or as members of professional and other communities when showing more respect for nature. As Joseph Stiglitz observes, companies can also be thought of as communities, people working together for a common purpose. As they work together they care about each other and the community in which they work. That community is becoming larger and larger; globalisation has made it as big as the world in which we all live.

The concept of corporate social responsibility (CSR) started out in a local context by bringing about a change in the mind-set of corporations to the realisation that their social image mattered. It had become generally accepted that people feel better and do a better job when working for a respected company than for one with a bad image. Better labour quality means better products and, in the end, a better financial result, both for shareholders and stakeholders. Building a good image has proven to be an important part of building brands.

This is by no means a new discovery, as the author points out in citing Adam Smith. This idea didn't come with CSR. Nor is it a policy agreed on by all and pursued with no exceptions. The trends might be in the right direction. Pressure from consumer demands and government legislation has played a role. So have the examples set by far-sighted business leaders at many levels and in many sectors. This is part of the changing business environment in which companies operate. Still there are just too many examples of how a combination of negligence and ignorance has resulted in serious damage to the environment and with it the reputation of business.

The author is in favour of extending the scope of CSR beyond its present limited reach to becoming the base for a global strategy. In the World Council for Corporate Governance (WCFCG) we talk about such a widening of the 'mandate' of CSR, as 'CSR plus', and Caleb Wall has been active in these debates. This development is influenced by the fact that climate change and other threats to the environment have resulted in entirely new challenges for everyone responsible for economic activities. The pressure on business to play a role in social issues, environmental protection and poverty alleviation among them, is bound to grow.

The type of thinking that business leaders are asked to indulge in when facing social issues, climate change and other symptoms of a stressed planet Earth is commonly labelled the 'triple bottom line'. This lists *people, planet* and *profit* as equally important concerns for business. This is a thinking that has its origin in CSR and it is based on hard economic facts. As highlighted in the UK's *Stern Review on the Economics of Climate Change*, unabated climate change in the future could cost the global economy 5–20 times more than the cost of reducing the emissions that are now causing global warming.

The business community listens carefully to warnings on how companies will be affected. Today, climate change and other environmental problems are no longer disputed phenomena but are scientifically well documented and commonly accepted facts.

Said one institution following the publication of the latest UN report on climate change: 'The pace of firms' adaptation to climate change over the next several years is likely to prove to be another of the forces that influence whether any given firm survives and prosper or withers and, quite possibly, dies.'

Said another: 'Policies to combat the threat of global warming are converging to influence people's behaviour, alter the risk profile of various businesses and improve the outlook for others.'

Even before climate change began to make front-page news there was a trend among investors of giving short-term profit lower priority than the need for long-term strategies of building brands and emphasising social responsibilities and ethical behaviour. As part of that trend corporations should not be seen only as economic entities but – still on business terms – as instruments of social and economic transformation, for the sake of society and business itself.

Corporations, big and small, are operating within an increasingly integrated world economy. If CSR as a tool or measurement of the quality of management and its impact on society isn't being adjusted to that development, it risks becoming obsolete beyond limited aspects of labour relations and local community affairs. When the WCFCG calls for 'CSR plus', the 'plus' stands for the global dimension of a business strategy. This is for protecting the environment, the alleviation of poverty, improving transparency and ethical standards.

This seems so much more justified since the business community heeded former UN Secretary-General Kofi Annan's invitation to become a partner in the UN Millennium Development Goals (MDGs). These goals range from halving extreme poverty, to stopping the spread of HIV/AIDS and guaranteeing universal primary education by 2015. The recognition that meeting these goals requires concerted action by governments, international donor and other organisations and civil society should be seen as part of the changing business climate that Caleb Wall calls for in this book.

This is why the participation of the private sector is so important. Development does not happen without economic growth, economic growth requires investments, which require the active involvement of small and large, national and multinational corporations to create jobs and income.

The private sector has always played that role. How well or not so well business has contributed to supporting the poor in building their livelihoods has depended on the attitude of the corporate sector and the success of governments in creating an enabling milieu for friendly investments. In other words: the *business climate*.

Progress has been made, but with close to 4 billion people living on less than US$2 a day there is a need for new thinking among all the partners in the MDG endeavour, business included. The business opportunities are many, as recent successes among the developing countries show. One approach should be to adjust product development, manufacturing, marketing and financing to meet the needs of the poor as consumers and to encourage entrepreneurship as a force for development.

This should be seen from the perspective of CSR and its implementation through governance at three levels: global, national and corporate.

The economies of many multinational companies are bigger than the economies of many small and medium-sized nations. Neither one will always be the best custodian of the environment. Both governments and corporations will at times (but not always) do their best to avoid rather than live up to their social responsibility. That's when weak governments are weak and corrupt and when corporations are poorly controlled.

With corporations so deeply involved in areas that were traditionally government responsibilities, a number of questions arise:

- On which principle do we define the limits of what today are considered to be areas of corporate responsibility?

- How far can or should that limit be stretched?

- How should corporations and/or their organisations relate to issues where the responsibility clearly rests with governments although with direct consequence for business?

Today the typical attitude of business is often too much one of 'oppose and accept'. Being against all kinds of new regulation has for the business communities become a cliché. Still, when new policies have been introduced, most industries seem both willing and able to adjust to the new conditions. The attitude of business to the Kyoto Protocol has been no exception. These are what the author describes as 'compliant corporations'.

That doesn't seem to me to be a particularly far-sighted and entrepreneurial policy. It is very likely that globalisation and global environmental challenges will force a change. The threat from climate change in nature will have to result in a *climate change in business*. What is needed is a shift from denial about what is obvious to a position of reason; from a defensive to a critical but proactive attitude; a new mind-set that would make business a partner in policy-making instead of always an opponent.

Still, the role of government and business should be kept apart. Governments should listen to business when setting the targets through framework legislation. Business should be trusted to find the best way, in terms of choosing technology and otherwise, to reach those targets. Markets alone cannot always deliver the right solutions. Government and business must learn how to work together.

Implementing good corporate governance in a globalised world, burdened as it is with global-scale problems, still presents many opportunities. But achieving this requires a useful guide to *implementing* CSR, and this is where Caleb Wall's book is of great interest.

Acknowledgements

I wish to thank all the participants in the case studies. Their inputs and experiences have made writing this book much more interesting and rewarding. Special thanks are due to Ola Ullsten (WCFCG), Nick Hart (Turner Europe), Corinne Adam (Gildan) and Jan Peter Bergkvist (Scandic Hotels) who supported the book from the earliest stages, as well as to Edward Bickham and Jonathan Samuel (Anglo American) for their help in the final stages, and launch, of the book.

I also wish to acknowledge the support of my family, friends and colleagues — their feedback and encouragement was invaluable.

— For Barbara —

1

The opportunity of corporate responsibility

Climate change and poverty are real problems and these problems are especially difficult in the 'hard' industries such as mining, oil, textiles and travel, for which solutions to social and environmental problems are not readily available or simple to implement. There is a growing political and social consensus that businesses, especially multinational corporations (MNCs), need to accept their share of responsibility for these problems. Yet too often companies are criticised for their role in causing these problems, without acknowledgement of the positive contributions companies make to the communities and environments in which they work. This book highlights the ways in which companies can create 'shared value'. This approach means that companies take corporate social responsibility (CSR) seriously, while seeing the opportunities that exist for growing their business, brands and markets by engaging in this challenge. Thus CSR is about enhancing profitability and building the company's brand; seeing CSR as an opportunity not a threat. CSR is not philanthropy; instead it is about companies ensuring that their core operations contribute to social development and environmental protection *as well as* expanding the business and growing profits.

The case for CSR is strong and businesses today are keen to engage in the social and environmental issues of our time. But what is often lacking is an understanding of *how to implement* CSR.

Achieving this requires a change in business climate, where companies place their social and environmental responsibilities at the core of their business decision-making. Likewise governments and non-governmental organisations (NGOs) need to play their role in shaping the business climate, with governments setting the right 'rules of the game' and NGOs engaging with businesses in a responsible and accountable manner. The key to this is partnership and cooperation, rather than antagonism, and all three actors have a role to play in successfully implementing CSR.

Much has been written telling companies to 'do' CSR, but a common complaint from my consultancy clients is that there is no book on *how* to go about CSR — especially for the more difficult industries where cheap and immediate fixes are not always available. Business leaders now accept that social goals are complementary to long-term business goals and that a responsibility for action lies with business. This is especially the case for companies working in 'dirty' industries and in the developing world — which calls for 'hard' CSR.

This book is an implementation guide on CSR for companies, big and small, working in the 'hard' industries and the developing world. The case studies help companies to understand *what* CSR is and *how* to put it at the core of their business decision-making.

Implementing corporate social responsibility

This book is based on case studies from a variety of companies across the business spectrum, demonstrating how CSR can be made to work in different circumstances. These cases are based on my visits to the site of operations and interviews with stakeholders, to document the benefits the company is bringing to local communities — but they are not my clients. These cases come from different industries; they include the very big and the very small but they all make CSR work in poverty-stricken areas of the world. What distinguishes these cases is that the companies were working in 'hard' industries — where CSR solutions were not immediately available — and that the companies concerned took a proactive approach to implementing CSR.

These companies are not perfect; some of them have arrived at their current policies by making mistakes in the past. But they have all made a commitment to CSR, which is now beginning to improve their business. They have had to make difficult decisions, balanced between competing priorities and these companies have had to engage their shareholders (and other stakeholders) in the debate. This has led to some very different approaches across the range of industries. Despite the differences between these companies we can distil six lessons from their operations on the key steps towards CSR in difficult industries:

1. Leverage your core competences

2. Collaborate based on common values

3. Operate globally–impact locally: creating opportunities for staff, suppliers and society

4. Use evolution and revolution: to change at every step along the value chain

5. Work with, rather than against, good governments

6. Cooperate with NGOs in a constructive way

This ongoing process can be visualised as a continuous cycle, as shown in Figure 1, all of which take place within a 'business climate' of constructive NGO and government collaboration.

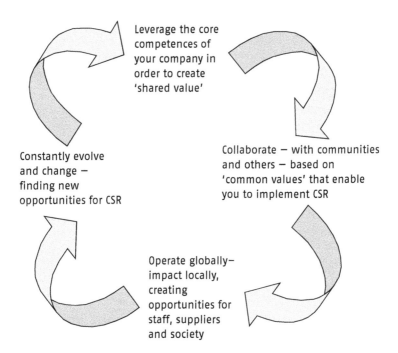

Leverage the core competences of your company in order to create 'shared value'

Collaborate – with communities and others – based on 'common values' that enable you to implement CSR

Constantly evolve and change – finding new opportunities for CSR

Operate globally–impact locally, creating opportunities for staff, suppliers and society

Figure 1 **Implementing CSR**

In this book I explain each of these concepts with a detailed case study to illustrate how a company has applied this in real life. The cases used include:

- **Leverage your core competences.** Anglo American's Zimele business development programme in South Africa

- **Collaborate based on common values.** Montana Exploradora and AMAC for community-based environmental management

- **Operate globally–impact locally.** Gildan, a major textile firm, conducting socially and environmentally responsible manufacturing in Honduras and Central America

- **Engage in constant evolution.** Scandic Hotels, implementing sustainability in an otherwise very polluting and unsustainable industry

- **Work with good governments.** Norway's waste in electrical and electronic items is managed using a pro-market, pragmatic solution, creating opportunities for profit and environmental protection

- **Cooperate with NGOs in a constructive way.** Turner Broadcasting Europe finding ways to use its core competences in partnership with NGOs

It is important to recognise that implementing CSR is a process. Good companies will continuously seek to find ways to improve on their performance and to use CSR to gain *strategic advantage* over the competition. In so doing they should also seek to find new ways to create value for staff and society and to protect the environment. Using core competences and collaboration with communities in this way is not a new idea: organisations such as the World Business Council for Sustainable Development have been instrumental in leading the 'core competence' movement in CSR (advocating a mix of Core Competences, Partnerships and Localisation in their field guide to 'Doing Business with the Poor' in 2004). What is new is the idea that these all work together in the context of government and NGO collaboration – a 'business climate change' – for companies working in difficult industries in different parts of the world. It is the combination of skills, competences, collaborations and constant changes – set out in practice in these case studies – that delivers local development and private profit. This is an approach I refer to as 'creating shared value'.

Shared value and common values

Underlying this approach is a view – an opinion based on experience – that companies perform best when they create 'shared value'. Shared value is about increasing long-term returns to shareholders (shareholder value) through invest-ing in value creation for staff, stakeholders, society and the environment. So implementing CSR is not about companies engaging in charity; on the contrary, it is about companies actively pursuing their self-interests but in the process creat-ing value for society.

This approach has been labelled 'proper selfishness' by Charles Handy (1997). It means moving beyond CSR as charity, towards seeing CSR as an investment. This can be termed a win–win situation. I call it creating 'shared value'; in many ways it is just good management. But, while the language of CSR may be new, the concept is not. Adam Smith discussed the concept in 1776:

> Every individual necessarily labours to render the annual revenue of the society as great as he can. He generally, indeed, neither intends to promote the public interest, nor knows how much he is promoting it . . . he intends only his own gain, and he is in this, as in many other cases, led by an invisible hand to promote an end which was no part of his intention. Nor is it always the worse for the society that it was no part of it. By pursuing his own interest he fre-quently promotes that of the society more effectually than when he really intends to promote it. I have never known much good done by those who affected to trade for the public good. *It is not from the benevolence of the butcher, the brewer, or the baker, that we expect our dinner, but from their regard to their own interest.* We address ourselves, not to their humanity but to their self-love, and never talk to them of our own necessities but of their advantages (Adam Smith, *Wealth of Nations*, 1776).

The challenge for the responsible company is to find ways in which the pursuit of shareholder interest also meets social interests. Companies that leverage their core competences, and put CSR at the core of their business model, do so in their own self-interest, but in doing so also benefit society. Reconciling the necessity of environmental protection – while distributing the advantages of economic growth – is key to understanding the opportunities for business in embracing CSR.

This concept is explained in Figure 2, which illustrates the ways in which busi-nesses, society and the environment already create shared value. The challenge, and the opportunity, is to move businesses, society and the environment more closely together – building on common interests and common values – to create greater shared value.

However, there will always be cases where the pursuit of private profit leads to public ill. Actions that pollute the environment, destroy natural capital or harm individuals' rights may well be profitable – but they are certainly not in the pub-

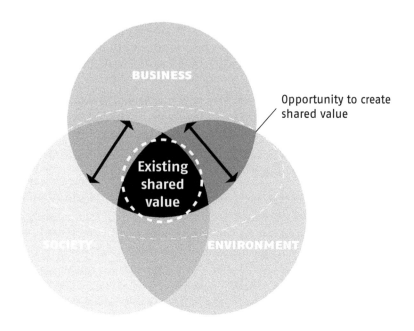

Figure 2 **Opportunities to create shared value**

lic good. This is where governments, in concert with businesses and NGOs, play a role in setting the 'rules of the game' within which companies need to operate. If activities that reduce the public good are made unprofitable – through taxation, legislation and popular pressure – then companies will cease to engage in them. The current situation, of publicly expecting companies to act responsibly but not punishing irresponsible companies, or punishing them insufficiently encourages a 'moral hazard'. This is where regulations need to follow the 'polluter pays principle' to ensure that there is a financial incentive for responsible corporate behaviour.

The point here is in making sure that irresponsible corporations do not gain a competitive advantage over responsible corporations (free-riding) and this can be achieved by changing the business environment in which companies operate. NGOs, governments and the public all have a role to play in this. However, companies should not wait for a change in the law in order for them to become responsible, as there are considerable opportunities in adopting CSR as a form of forward thinking management.

In addition, we also see that behind these successes are good government policies that encourage companies and NGOs to act in a responsible manner. These partnerships and collaborations need to be founded on *common values*: that is, shared definitions of the problems at hand and common understandings of how to address these issues. Having common values, shared goals and understandings is crucial to working in partnership with NGOs, governments and society.

The following chapters deal with how shared value can be created by implementing CSR. But first it is important to give some background on CSR, the social and environmental problems that face us today and the opportunities for action.

A brief history of corporate social responsibility

The idea that companies and businesses contribute to society is not new. Indeed, in many cultures the concept of business is inseparable from the society in which it works.[1] In Western democracies there has always been a 'privileged place of business': an acceptance that economic growth and development are driven by companies and business people. This importance of business has led to certain privileges being enjoyed by business leaders: access to politicians, honours, awards and status. With these privileges have come responsibilities or *noblesse oblige*.[2]

This is not to contradict the 'business of business is business' approach, as outlined by Milton Friedman (1962), who stated that:

> There is one and only one social responsibility of business — to use its resources and engage in activities designed to increase its profits so long as it stays within the rules of the game, which is to say, engages in open and free competition without deception or fraud.

Rather, it emphasises that companies need to use their resources (here we call them core competences) and engage in activities to increase profits — but that this needs to be done within the 'rules of the game'. The reality is that the 'rules of the game' are changing.

As large corporations have grown in power and influence, so too has the social and political consensus that companies need to accept responsibility for social and environmental problems, especially those that can be directly tied to the operations of the company. This responsibility goes beyond following the law (although this is essential) and it is distinct from charity or philanthropic activities; instead, it is about *how* companies conduct their business, taking responsibility for the impacts on society and the environment. In different markets this has taken different forms. Consumer goods retailing has tended to focus on specific issues along the supply chain: child labour, food miles and ethical sourcing.

In other industries with less consumer appeal, such as the construction industry, CSR has yet to take hold. Meanwhile, some 'dirty' industries — especially the extractives — have faced considerable pressure to change their practices and considerable scepticism about the impact of the changes they have put in place.

Since the 1960s and 1970s, it has been recognised that the activities of businesses have negative as well as positive impacts on society and the environment. In the United States, in particular, corporate reports began to include comments on the environmental impact that companies were making. In these early years, much of this was little more than a public relations exercise, with the companies making non-binding commitments to environmental protection, with no clear link to business practice. These 'greenwash' reports were seldom informative and often backfired (Tepper Marlin and Tepper Marlin 2003), especially in the face of the growing strength and public profile of NGOs such as Greenpeace. Public pressure began to mount on companies to be held accountable for their actions and these pressures grew during the 1970s with a loss of faith by the public in their political and economic leaders. The 'greenwash' reports were no longer sufficient. The public demanded action and governments moved towards a general (and sometimes seemingly indiscriminate) toughening of the regulatory environment, forcing firms to be proactive in their reporting. Faced with government regulation, some businesses chose to be proactive. These new challenges presaged the 'stakeholder' approach to corporate reporting.

Corporate reporting

In 1989 Ben & Jerry's, a North American ice cream manufacturer, began a new phase of corporate reporting. It provided not only financial reports aimed at shareholders, but also a 'Stakeholders Report' that detailed the firm's relationships with its stakeholders: communities, employees, customers, suppliers and investors (Tepper Marlin and Tepper Marlin 2003). This approach to reporting on a firm's social and environmental impact was new, ushering in a decade of initiatives aimed at the accurate reporting of company responsibilities. The 1990s saw a number of companies take the lead in voluntary reporting of how they were meeting their corporate social responsibilities. Because of the wide variety of different social and environmental impacts that firms have, across different industries and in different parts of the world, comparison of CSR reports is more difficult than traditional financial reports.

Certain common standards do exist for reporting, yet it remains difficult, even today, to adequately compare companies across (or even within) industries. There are also some enduring questions on how 'sustainable' triple-bottom-line and other CSR reporting is — given the variability of results and difficulties in defining common standards. A useful discussion of this problem can be found in *The*

Triple Bottom Line: Does It All Add Up? Assessing the Sustainability of Business and CSR edited by Adrian Henriques and Julie Richardson (2004). In an effort to provide clarity, common standards have been established, such as:

- AccountAbility's AA1000 standard, based on triple-bottom-line reporting (people, planet, profits)

- Global Reporting Initiative's Sustainability Reporting Guidelines

- Social Accountability International's SA8000 standard

- The ISO 14000 environmental management standard

These new voluntary reporting requirements were not necessarily an added obligation for firms; they also provided opportunities for profit. The Body Shop built much of its corporate brand in the 1990s on the basis of its approach to animal testing and environmentally friendly manufacturing, processing and packaging. Indeed, the stock market valuation of companies is increasingly driven by CSR reporting.

Analysts are recognising that well-run companies, with a long-term, strategic perspective, are also those companies that are proactive in stakeholder reporting. Recent research is highlighting the relationship between corporate social and environmental performance and corporate financial performance (see, for example, Rowe 2005 and Orlitzky *et al.* 2003). This research shows how well-managed firms, which are active in stakeholder reporting, exhibit superior returns and profitability. Because these companies are aware of their social and environmental responsibilities, and — just as important — because they are being strategic in addressing these responsibilities, their market value is improved. While financial reporting remains crucial, there is an awareness that: 'Even from a strict shareholder-value perspective, most stock market value — typically over 80% in American and western European public markets — depends on expectations of companies' cash flow beyond the next three years' (Davis 2005).

From this long-term perspective there is recognition that CSR reporting is a good indicator of long-term fiscal performance as well as an adequate proxy for good corporate governance. In this way CSR reporting has moved from being 'greenwash' towards being a central part of business reporting. Because of this recognition, and as a result of considerable public pressure, companies have begun to engage in CSR — but the forms that this has taken have not always been strategic or well thought through.

Corporate social charity

Having spent the 1990s reporting on their social and environmental impacts, companies have also adopted CSR policies and procedures. This has seen CSR progress from being a fringe activity, carried out by a few firms, to a necessary part of a company's annual reporting. Few major companies today fail to have a section of their website or reports dedicated to CSR. But, despite this progress into the public consciousness, most CSR policies fail to move beyond charity. That is because CSR activities are notionally a 'cost' that the company spends, as opposed to seeing opportunities for profit. The downside of this is that it does not create shared value for the company and stakeholders, which is the real opportunity of CSR.

If we analyse some of what passes for CSR today we begin to see two broad trends: for actions that companies should be taking anyway and for activities that could be classified as charity. The first group consists of activities and initiatives that well-run companies should be engaging in already. Whether this is installing low-energy lighting, saving money on packaging and transport or reducing staff turnover through better health and safety, companies should be taking these initiatives already. Because these are cost-cutting measures that also incidentally have an environmental or social good, it is stretching the definition of CSR to include any cost-saving initiative. Of course, creating win–win solutions is central to strategic CSR, as demonstrated below. But CSR does and will entail tough choices: responsible corporations need to do more than just adhere to current laws and regulations; sometimes taking a lead will have a short-term cost. The challenge is in plotting a strategy that furthers the *long-term* interests of shareholders while also enhancing value for stakeholders, staff and society.

This is where the other common variant of CSR today is somewhat more pernicious. Large companies donating a small fraction of their profits to charity, and calling this CSR, is certainly common. Often this is couched as a large sum of money — indeed it is — but as a fraction of the company's profits it is often derisory. More important than the figure, say 1% of pre-tax profits, is the question of how the company is generating the other 99% of profits. If these profits come from degrading the environment and damaging communities and society, then 1% of the profits will not reduce this damage. Certainly, some charitable giving and some foundations do excellent work. But we need to see this much more for what it really is: charity. In helping to secure a company's licence to operate this might be money well spent, but the impact is inevitably limited if companies are not engaged in how the money is spent. This is where there are some real opportunities, to take the good intentions and funding currently dedicated to charitable giving, and to target these more strategically. By engaging staff and the company's core competences, a greater impact can be had without reducing (indeed, hopefully also enhancing) returns to shareholders. This is where we can stop talking about CSR as charity and begin identifying the opportunities of CSR.

Corporate social opportunity?

The 'state of the art' in CSR is to see the opportunities for business engaging fully with its social and environmental responsibilities. Plenty of books tell us of the *Corporate Social Opportunity!* (Grayson and Hodges 2004) for *Doing the Most Good for Your Company and Your Cause* (Kotler and Lee 2005), some even suggest that we *Make Poverty Business: Increase Profits and Reduce Risks by Engaging with the Poor* (Wilson and Wilson 2006). Many of these books provide good examples of how some companies, especially those selling to the 'bottom of the pyramid' (BOP) have made a fortune by making their products available to the poorest consumers (Prahalad 2004).

These examples are useful, but I think it is inaccurate to suggest that, for every company, working in every market, there is a set of clear steps that can easily turn responsibilities into opportunities. For most companies, operating in fiercely competitive markets where it is often difficult to gain brand differentiation, the usual arguments in favour of CSR are somewhat weak. This is where the current approach to CSR is flawed. The initial discussion of 'corporate social responsibility' put companies in a defensive posture, where they were expected to spend money on charity and philanthropy, in addition to their existing social commitments. Likewise, by discussing CSR people often ignore the environmental responsibilities of companies, which is why I use CSR to encompass the full range of corporate responsibilities — social, environmental and ethical.

At present, as much as companies issue sustainability and stakeholder reports, CSR remains a part of the firm's overall publicity or marketing policy. What is needed instead is a move of CSR towards the centre of company strategy. As important as it is for firms to publicise the contributions they already make to society (employment, investment in innovation, supporting new technologies), it is more useful for the company to engage in the social and environmental challenges that have an impact on their business. This is more than a simple accounting or reporting of the company's impact on the environmental issue of present popularity. Rather, companies should compete to find different approaches to solving the social and environmental challenges that face their particular business (which is why I argue for leveraging core competences in the next chapter), deriving their comparative advantage from how well they work with stakeholders to address these issues. I next set out what some of these specific challenges are and some of the opportunities for action that exist.

But it would also be wrong to assume that every company can simply use their core competences to do good. CSR is not always that easy. Some industries are inherently polluting to the environment and a few industries are inherently damaging to the public good. While we should not rush to condemn these industries, as they also tend to create public good and provide essential goods and services, we need to be realistic about how much public benefit they create. Take, for example, the oil industry, which undoubtedly has a negative environmental impact and often works in unhealthy political societies. Yet energy is essential for human existence, everyone uses these products and the world would be substantively worse off without the oil industry.

The challenge for the oil industry is to do *as good a job as possible* of cleanly and efficiently extracting oil, while also using their core skills to improve the societies and environments in which they work. They must also — as we are beginning to see with BP, Shell and others — invest their skills and expertise in creating future energy solutions that do not have the same environmental impacts. As a long-term strategy this should also be seen as a smart investment in sustainable profits — as well as a responsible effort to meet today's social and environmental challenges.

But in doing this companies need to remain focused on their core business and doing this better. BP's efforts at moving 'Beyond Petroleum' were seriously undermined by a spate of safety problems and pipeline leakages in its North American operations. Efforts to become a responsible corporation should not distract managers from ensuring that existing responsibilities — to staff, shareholders and the environment — are met. In his book *Supercapitalism*, Robert Reich (2007) denounces CSR as a dangerous diversion from the proper focus of firms — on producing goods and services that enhance the public good. This is perhaps a useful antidote to the current trend in CSR, towards crediting corporations as being 'socially responsible' if they take any effort towards improving their environmental or social performance. This, Reich notes: 'is to stretch the term [CSR] to mean anything a company might do to increase profits if, in doing so, it also happens to have some beneficent impact on the rest of society' (Reich 2007).

This is why I advocate a balanced approach, mediating between meeting the interests of shareholders while *also* addressing a company's responsibilities to staff, stakeholders, society and the environment. As we see below, these challenges are considerable and they are growing — which is why strategic CSR is so crucial to solving the major social and environmental challenges facing us today.

Social and environmental challenges

Global inequalities and global environmental problems are real, they are getting worse and in some cases their scale and impacts threaten the very ability of companies to continue operating in the manner to which they are accustomed. Some of these problems are caused by corporations, some are not. But the issue of initial responsibility for the problems needs to be distinguished from the common and shared responsibility for action. As global problems, those countries and companies that are rich enough to confront poverty and environmental degradation have both an *obligation* and an *interest* in confronting these problems. The obligation is a moral one, it has been well written about elsewhere and it is ultimately the decision of each individual how they deal with this obligation. What I wish to discuss is how confronting poverty and environmental degradation is in the best interests of business – for medium-term profitability and long-term viability.

Rather than talk about issues such as climate change and inequality in the abstract, it is more useful to show a few examples of what this means for real people and real companies. The following examples are indicative; they are not exhaustive. But what they each illustrate is the opportunities for action and the risks of inaction.

What poverty really means

One billion people, one-sixth of the world's population, live in 'deep poverty' (World Bank 2007). This is poverty that is deeper and more persistent than the US$1 per day that is usually defined as a global indicator of poverty. Instead, 'deep poverty' means living on less than half of the officially defined poverty level. In some countries this is a matter of cents per day, in reality it is a matter of calories a day. Whether cents or calories, it is never enough, trapping people in a cycle of poverty from which they cannot break free. Daily life, for the 1 billion people in deep poverty, is about survival. The idea that this is an untapped market, at the 'bottom of the pyramid' is naive. Such a BOP market does exist, among the working poor and low-income earners in under-served economies. But those in deep poverty are not a potential market for consumer goods, nor is it right to talk in such terms when people are starving. But the 1 billion people in deep poverty are a potential business risk and – despite their lack of purchasing power – are potential business partners for businesses with sufficiently long-term horizons.

Deep poverty is problematic. It raises serious security risks for business operations. It calls into question the 'licence to operate' of businesses and the legitimacy of governments.[3] It drives social problems such as crime, illegal migration, the spread of disease and is an acknowledged cause of terrorism. These social problems make doing business, especially in the poorest parts of the world, less secure and more expensive. So it is in the *interest* of businesses to contribute to alleviating deep poverty. Not because there is a potential market there (although in the long run this could be the case) but because poverty undermines the legitimacy of businesses and increases business costs. This is not to apportion blame. Deep poverty is not caused by businesses; in fact some of the greatest contributions to poverty alleviation have come about with the help of business:

It is clear from the experience of countries that have been most successful in reducing poverty — Japan, China, Singapore, South
Korea, and Botswana, for instance — that the creation of profitable
businesses is the key. They provide the jobs, income, and motivation for education and individual development that raise standards
of living (Lodge and Wilson 2007).

Governments must continue to take the lead in combating poverty, through
official development assistance, as well as through constructive engagement with
businesses, NGOs and the multilateral agencies. Yet businesses still hold a
responsibility to address deep poverty wherever it is in the world. Global companies can no longer hide from their social responsibilities. In fact, it is in their
interests to engage in the problem of deep poverty, both to ensure their own
'licence to operate' and to reduce the business risks that come with the existence
of poverty.

Global change: local impact

Human-induced global warming is now accepted. Business leaders, politicians
and the public are finally convinced by what scientists have been saying for the
past 20 years — that the Earth is warming and that human activity is the likely
cause. The projected impacts of this global warming — a 1-metre sea-level rise,
increased incidence of extreme weather events, a 1–3°C rise in average tempera-
tures — belie the local impact that these global changes will have. Bangladesh, one
of the world's poorest countries, stands to lose 17.5% of its land area if there is a 1-
metre sea-level rise. The United States, one of the world's richest countries, stands
to lose 26,000 km² of dry land if sea level rises by 0.6 metres.

The increased incidence of extreme weather events will make the long supply
chains of the globalised economy more susceptible to strains; disruptive events
will become more common and more costly. Temperature rises will coincide with
regional climatic variations — more floods *and* more droughts — making food supplies less reliable and more expensive.

Business as usual cannot and will not continue.

This argument is well made in the UK's *Stern Review*,[4] which analyses the economics of climate change from the business perspective. What Sir Nicholas Stern
found is that unabated climate change could cost the global economy from 5% to
20% of GDP each year, whereas the cost of reducing emissions could be limited to
around 1% of global GDP, as a one-off charge. So taking action is not a case of charity or business expense; it is an investment in future productivity and even in the
viability of the global economic system. This is where the current approach, of

'offsetting' carbon by buying credits, is perhaps slightly wrong-headed. Carbon dioxide emissions damage the environment and, as a result, the long-term viability of most countries and companies. Buying CO_2 offsets helps to balance the overall carbon impact of operations, but not nearly as much as genuine CO_2 reductions do. Equally, buying offsets on a voluntary basis enables less ethical companies to become more profitable – a dilemma discussed later in this book. What is needed is an effort by responsible companies to reduce their CO_2 emissions, combined with businesses engaging with governments to make emissions trading compulsory rather than voluntary – thus ensuring that compliant corporations also reduce their emissions. This approach would likely have greater benefits for the environment as a whole, while avoiding the 'free-rider' dilemma of voluntary schemes.

Moreover, it is a wise investment: shifting the world onto a 'low-carbon' path could benefit the global economy by US$2,500 billion a year, including a market for low-carbon technologies that could be worth US$500 billion by 2050.[5] Such an investment is not only socially responsible, but it represents a responsible investment of shareholder funds by any business in long-term profitability. Yet, even if these investments are made, global warming will continue (due to the existing 'stock' of emissions), and companies will have to adapt to these changes, especially in dealing with the local impacts of this global change. How companies respond to this challenge will define the legitimacy and longevity of companies in the future.

Oil oases in rural Kazakhstan

Kazakhstan, a vast post-Soviet republic in Central Asia, has tremendous natural resources. As one of the fastest-growing suppliers of oil and gas, with vast agricultural lands and significant deposits of ferrous and precious metals, Kazakhstan has the resources to be a wealthy country. Yet rural poverty in Kazakhstan affects 31% of the population, with some of the most oil-rich districts experiencing upwards of 40% of the population in poverty.[6] Disturbingly, Kazakhstan is beginning to show signs of the 'resource curse' with a high exchange rate, low investment in non-energy sectors and rising unemployment (Wall 2007). The extractive industries invested heavily in Kazakhstan after independence in 1991; companies such as Chevron, ENI and others entered joint ventures to explore and extract oil, gas and minerals. This investment is capital-intensive, it requires skilled labour and much of the benefit of this investment flows out from the rural areas, towards the main cities and abroad. While rising income inequality is a natural corollary of the transition from a socialist to a market economy, more problematic has been the increase in power inequality:

> Much of the opprobrium attaching to income inequality is actually
> a dislike of the inequalities in power and influence that go with it.
> In undemocratic societies there is little difference between income
> and power: the rich rule and the rulers make themselves rich. The
> poor are powerless and exploited . . . Income inequalities may be
> justified on the grounds that incentives are needed to encourage
> hard work and entrepreneurship. There is no comparable justifica-
> tion for power inequalities.[7]

Local resentment of this inequality of power is exacerbated by a collapsing rural
economy. The decline of Soviet collective farms was followed by a botched pri-
vatisation programme, with land and other agricultural assets appropriated by
elites. Rural healthcare and education are in a state of decline, characterised by
underinvestment and malaise. This is leading to greater inequalities between the
minority of 'new' urban citizens of Kazakhstan who have benefited from the
resources boom, and the majority who have seen their livelihoods decline.
National economic development has been hindered by the 'resource curse'
which has led to underinvestment in rural infrastructure.

This rural poverty and resentment now poses the greatest business risk to companies operating in Kazakhstan. Riots and protests, directed against foreign
labour in the construction sector, are but one indicator of popular dissatisfaction.
The risk this poses to the companies working there, for the security of their staff
and operations, as well as the risk of forced shutdowns, is considerable. Multi-
million-dollar investments are under threat because of the rural poverty that
exists in Kazakhstan. Whether companies caused this poverty or not, the risk –
and therefore responsibility and cost – falls on them. This is where investments
in rural infrastructure and community development can pay dividends for
responsible corporations. By localising supply chains, mobilising rural employment and investing in shared transport infrastructure, companies can trim down
their business costs, while reducing their political risk by promoting social development. By providing the rural population with employment opportunities,
with a stake in a brighter future, the extractive industries have the potential to
create shared value.

Confronting challenges

The important point to note from these three examples is that companies,
whether or not they are the direct cause of the problems, have a vested interest in
alleviating these problems. The case for companies being held accountable for
their own direct environmental impacts is taken for granted. For companies, and
individuals, compliance with national and international law is mandatory. Experience has shown that companies do best to play a role in policy formulation,

rather than adopting an 'oppose and then accept' stance to government regulation.[8] The discussion on CSR deals with the extent to which companies should be
proactive in confronting the challenges that face society. In the case of global
poverty and climate change, the option of 'doing nothing' is no longer viable.
Rather, it is a question of what action companies will take and acknowledging that
these decisions will have long-term implications on the planet and on profits. For
more immediate, local, problems there is also a necessity for action. But the science and evidence is often partial. Thus it is important to understand the 'principles' of CSR, rather than trying to make a single CSR formula fit every different situation.

We see in the following chapters of this book how different companies have
identified the social and environmental problems that face their company and
stakeholders. The approach they took was determined by how the companies
and stakeholders perceived the problem and how they wished to respond to it.
Their actions reflect the specific skills and responsibilities of the company. There
is no formula or single 'right way' to be a responsible corporation. Just as businesses differentiate their products and compete in the marketplace, so too should
companies compete at CSR. In doing this it is useful to map corporate social
responsibility along a continuum, from the irresponsible to the responsible corporation. In Figure 3 we see how companies move towards higher levels of
responsible behaviour.

Figure 3 **Continuum of corporate social responsibility**

If you are reading this book, compliance with national laws is probably something you already do in your business. The question is how you move beyond
compliance to a proactive stance, aiming to take environmental and social leadership. The four lessons of the following chapters will help you apply the principles of CSR to your individual business and set of responsibilities. To help you

understand how different companies have different responsibilities and opportunities for action I detail below a set of four opportunities that exist for the responsible corporation.

Opportunities for action

The modern corporation has four key sets of responsibilities. These responsibilities also give us the framework of the opportunities for action in CSR. We can summarise these responsibilities as obligations to: shareholders, stakeholders, society and environment. The key here is to create 'shared value' for each of these groups. Different businesses, operating in different markets, will have different weighting of their responsibilities. The extractive industries have special obligations to environmental protection and, given the political climates they operate in, to the political health of society. Equally well, service companies will focus more on their responsibilities to stakeholders, with whom they have the greatest impact and strongest business interests (by building their brands). This reinforces the point that there is no 'right' approach to CSR. Companies need to tailor their CSR policies and practice based on their core competences and the opportunities to create shared value. This where the implementation guide given in this book is useful. It allows companies to use their core competences to meet the unique demands of the industry and geography in which they are working.

In implementing CSR, the ranking of responsibilities must remain in the correct order. This order of priorities can be visualised as concentric circles of influence and responsibility, set out in Figure 4. At the core are the investors, to whom the company is legally bound. But the business could not exist without its stakeholders, who form the next 'layer' of responsibilities. Equally, without a vibrant society and a healthy environment, business would be meaningless, so it is in the interests of the company to consider these factors.

Shareholders

The primary obligation of businesses is to their owners. Some writers try to argue that companies have their main obligation to their staff, to society or to the environment. I disagree. Businesses exist, primarily, to serve their owners, the obligation of managers is to maximise investor returns and the job of staff is to create wealth for the business. But in maximising returns it is crucial to look beyond the next quarterly result, further into the future, and this is where corporate social responsibility comes in. CSR is about maximising investor returns, by investing in social development and environmental sustainability, which determine the

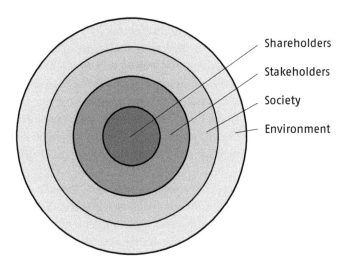

Shareholders

Stakeholders

Society

Environment

Figure 4 **Circles of influence and responsibility**

long-term financial returns of companies. This does not discount the importance of social and environmental obligations; rather, it places them in the correct order of priorities, with investor return as the most important. But there is no contradiction in investing in CSR; in fact, a proactive CSR policy is one of the best investments a company can make.

The financial markets already recognise this. Analysts are beginning to consider environmental, social and governance factors into their decision-making process, seeing that these variables can have a real impact on financial risk and return. For companies in the fast-moving consumer goods market, this is by accessing the 'fortune at the bottom of the pyramid'. For other industries the link is less clear, but it is just as important. The key aspect in the 'business climate change' approach to CSR is in recognising that CSR is about improving investor returns. This is only possible if CSR ceases being a business cost, part of the public relations (PR) budget, but instead is seen as an investment.

Managers need to be accountable for (long-term) returns on investments in CSR, but they also need to deliver short-term financial results. Finding the right balance between 'Tomorrow's Sustainability and Today's Profitability' is not necessarily easy, as Hawkins (2006) notes. In some cases these two are easy to reconcile, such as when: 'companies sometimes find ways to cut costs that coincide with what CSR activists want: Wal-Mart adopts cheaper "green" packaging, say, or Starbucks gives part-time employees health insurance, which reduces staff turnover' (*The Economist* 2007a).

But this is not always the case. Trade-offs are required and this is where it is useful to acknowledge that profitability and social good are not always aligned. Arguments about the 'correct' level of social engagement of businesses is changing all the time, with useful academic and public debates shaping this changing business landscape.[9] It is wrong to try to draw a particular line in the sand and stick to it. Instead I advocate acknowledging the *primary* responsibility of companies to create value for shareholders, without ignoring the *shared responsibility* to protect the environment and build healthy societies. Resolving the correct balance of these is best left, I believe, to the democratic institutions and political systems of the countries in which we live. At a wider level countries need to decide how to govern and regulate — how to set the business climate — in which companies compete.

Within corporations, competing opportunities for CSR must be weighed in terms of return on capital in the same way that other business decisions are made. Those companies that innovate and successfully implement CSR policies are the companies that will create improved investor returns, allowing them to continue in business and to carry on fulfilling their obligations to their stakeholders, the environment and society. This is where proactive and responsible corporations will play a role in helping to shape the changing business climate in which they operate.

Stakeholders

Investors, while the most important group, are not the only people with an interest in company performance. Stakeholders, people who are directly and indirectly involved in the business, are also important. Stakeholders play an important role in determining business performance and have a legitimate interest in, but not ownership of, the company. Again a hierarchy of importance is useful, with staff and customers as the most important stakeholders, followed by suppliers and finally by those affected by business operations, even if they are not directly involved.

In a democratic society, we recognise that people have a right to have a say in decisions that impact their lives. With the growing size and importance of large corporations and the emergence of business in areas formerly thought the domain of governments, there is a risk of a 'democratic deficit'. Much of the discontent expressed in anti-globalisation protests is about a lack of a say over decisions that affect people's lives. If people feel powerless, excluded and ignored, they have no option other than to protest and little to lose by doing so. The costs to business can be high when this happens. Selective boycotts, mass protests and (dis)information campaigns can be very harmful to company brands and sales. Often these campaigns are selective, targeting the biggest or most visible company without regard for the merits of each case. Witness the attacks on Nike (for child labour), McDonald's (fatty fast foods) and Starbucks (unethical coffee supplies); in each of these cases the company has been targeted, hurting profits and damaging brand value. This presents a real risk to businesses and profitability.

The good news is that stakeholders, if they are informed and given a say in decision-making, can contribute to the company rather than attack it. This is where collaborations based on common values (Chapter 3) are a powerful tool for companies to manage their risk. By harnessing the energy and resources of stakeholders, businesses can innovate more effectively, create new business opportunities and ensure their 'licence to operate'. Some governments already acknowledge this in their corporate law, requiring worker representation on boards, whereas some companies choose to appoint independent directors to represent stakeholder interests; these initiatives are to be commended. What's more, they help the company. Graduates compete to work for respected companies that respect them, suppliers want to sell to responsible partners and, most importantly, customers are loyal to those companies and brands that they respect. This is the real opportunity of CSR for improving profits.

Society

Society, the communities and countries in which companies conduct their business, are crucial to business. Businesses could not exist without healthy political systems to regulate the market, ensure security, enforce contracts and provide the rule of law. Companies have an interest, and responsibility, to engage in creating healthy societies and political systems. It is no coincidence that those countries that create the most wealth, are open to trade and have transparent capital markets, also have open political systems – as explained by George Soros (2000).

Corruption undermines political systems, preventing economic development and leading to the misallocation of resources.[10] Companies already have a legal obligation not to pay bribes, legal instruments that are backed up by mechanisms to prevent 'freeloaders' such as the Extractive Industries Transparency Initiative. But I would argue that it is also in companies' interests not to pay bribes or subvert society, as it reduces long-term economic development and thus diminishes long-term profitability. This is not so much an issue of self-regulation, as of self-restraint.

It is difficult to draw the line on what areas of social development companies should engage in. Should businesses operating in repressive regimes support opposition parties? Should companies take public stances on issues outside of their remit? These lines are fluid, but that does not mean that there are no limits to what is proper behaviour. Companies need to recognise and respect the supremacy of democratic governments. Engagement in democratic debate is fine, but attempts to wield power *over* the democratic system are unacceptable. Sir Mark Moody-Stuart, former chairman of the Royal Dutch/Shell Group (and current Chairman of Anglo American plc), in a keynote address to the International

Institute for Sustainable Development, explained how he dealt with this conundrum, when it was:

> once suggested to me that it was my (and Shell's) responsibility to raise with the US government the issue of the death penalty in the US. Although I personally am opposed to the death penalty, and would vote against it in my own country, and would express this opinion if asked, I do not think that our corporate responsibility extends to this.[11]

Sir Mark is right. Companies have an obligation, and interest, in supporting human rights and the growth of healthy societies. But how a company does this is crucial. Firms must wield their power in a constructive and responsible manner, which is likely to have a positive impact. Companies can often do this by requiring their local partners (including government owned partners) to comply with their corporate policies; they can do it through partnerships with representatives of 'civil society' (NGOs): again the specific solution is different for each company. The crucial point is in recognising the interest of the company in engaging with society in a responsible manner.

Environment

The natural environment supports all aspects of human life. It is naive to pretend that businesses could operate without a healthy environment and it is accepted that companies have a large (and growing) impact on the state of the environment. The idea of a change in business climate is to alter the way in which companies, and governments, see the environment. Until recently companies have been able to 'externalise' the true costs of their pollution, by polluting within certain guidelines and to certain limits. The key to solving this is not just in voluntary schemes, in which some leading companies hurt their profits by being more responsible than others.

In environmental problems, the 'free-rider' phenomenon means that regulation and proper markets for pollution are essential. In some cases voluntary schemes do work, especially as proactive corporations lead the way forward. Thus, a mixture of approaches and policies is required.[12] When the true price of environmental degradation is calculated, companies can then compete and innovate to reduce their costs (and therefore pollution). Changing the business climate is not about stopping businesses from doing what it is they are best at, rather it is about harnessing the power of the market, to protect the environment. But this does not mean that companies will be worse off.

The *Stern Review* calculates that there is US$85 worth of damage caused by every tonne of CO_2 emitted, but that emissions can be cut for less than US$25 per tonne.

As the financial incentives to diversify into 'carbon-neutral' business grow, so too will the profits for leading companies. Again this is not a matter of weighing business *against* the environment. Instead it is a case of recognising that, without a healthy environment, business is not possible in the long run. Economic growth will only be sustained if it is accompanied by sustainable development.

The key is in changing the business climates in which companies operate, encouraging innovation and conservation. In poor countries, where regulation is weak and enforcement poor, voluntary approaches by leading companies are showing how it is possible to reconcile the seemingly contradictory pressures of planet and profits. For international problems, such as climate change, a mixture of voluntary and compulsory approaches is showing great promise. Excessive regulation risks stifling innovation, but incentives are required to make voluntary schemes work. Businesses need to work with — not against — good governments, communities and their stakeholders in addressing environmental problems; it is within their sphere of influence and is very much in their long-term interest.

Conclusions

Corporate social responsibility is no longer an optional part of doing business. The scale of the global challenges that confront us today mean that businesses have a *responsibility* and an *interest* in confronting these challenges. The question for business leaders, for readers of this book, is how to respond to this challenge. The choice is between an 'oppose and then accept' approach, waiting for governments to take regulatory action and then working within these boundaries, and taking a proactive stance, helping to define the debate and play a role in shaping the regulations that govern your business. In doing this companies can find new business opportunities, build their brand and expand markets.

It is in the interests of business to be proactive. Long-term profitability, the most important responsibility of management, can only be assured by taking an active stance on CSR. Businesses need to engage in the social and environmental problems of today, to ensure their viability tomorrow. The case studies in the following chapters demonstrate how a proactive approach has allowed companies to turn their obligations into opportunities. Business leaders, politicians and civil society need to work towards a new business climate which puts corporate social responsibility at the heart of business strategy and decision-making.

Leverage your core competences

The business of business is business. It is not the job of companies to get involved in activities outside of their mandate and markets. But, by taking their social and environmental responsibilities seriously, companies can improve profitability while contributing to the public good – especially when working in poor markets and developing countries. This is what I call creating 'shared value' for shareholders and society. If we go back to the idea of the circles of influence and responsibility in Figure 4, the main business of business is in creating wealth for shareholders.

But business responsibilities and opportunities extend beyond this. They include the benefits of engaging with employees, suppliers and society and the necessity of confronting environmental issues such as climate change as global problems. Part of this is a mind-shift from seeing the pursuit of profit and protecting the environment as opposing ideals, recognising instead the reality that businesses are stakeholders in the environment.[13] Thus protecting the environment, and helping to build healthy societies, is in the shared interests of shareholders and wider society. I argue that the best way for businesses to serve these interests is by leveraging their core competences.

Businesses are good at creating employment, at finding new ways to improve productivity, at creating new markets and building wealth around the globe.

Businesses are not good at operating social programmes (unless that is their specific mandate), at engaging in operations outside of their 'licence to operate' or at regulating themselves. When considering how to engage in corporate social responsibility, companies need first to understand their own core competences. For some firms it will be their ability to create and manage intellectual capital, for others their core competence (CC) lies in their ability to invest and manage risk in difficult environments. Your core competence is what gives your company a comparative advantage over other companies. It is perhaps the most valuable part of your business and it should be leveraged wherever possible. CSR is about harnessing these core competences in a way that benefits the company and the community by creating shared value. In this way *implementing* CSR can be seen as a responsible investment in future returns (shareholder value) which also creates value for staff, stakeholders, society and the environment.

We see later in this chapter the case study of Anglo American and its 'Zimele' – or Independence through Enterprise – programme in South Africa. This initiative is clearly aimed at using the core technical and business skills of Anglo American, leveraging these in a way that helps promote local economic development and entrepreneurialism, while also helping to make the supply chain more flexible and robust. By contributing business acumen, helping to leverage finance and technical advice, Anglo American is able to contribute to the development of healthy and prosperous communities in the mining regions in which it works. This in turn enhances the company's licence to operate and helps it demonstrate its positive contribution to the country – an issue of increasing importance in an era of resource nationalism. This link, between creating value for society and enhancing shareholder value, shows how in many ways implementing CSR is good management.

CSR as good management

It is no accident that those companies that voluntarily took a proactive approach to CSR in the 1990s – Ben & Jerry's, Timberland Shoes, Indian Tobacco Corporation – have enjoyed superior stock market results. This is because, in pursuing CSR, these companies were pursuing their own self-interest. There is nothing wrong with this; in fact, this is exactly the sort of 'proper selfishness' that Charles Handy talks about: an active self-interest which also benefits society and protects the environment. But it would be naive to suggest that every company that has performed well on the stock market has also fulfilled its social and environmental responsibilities. Likewise, there is more to gauging a company's contribution

Figure 5 **Profits and public good: the CSR matrix**

to society than a simple glance at the balance sheet — hence the introduction of triple-bottom-line accounting. But what we can say is that, in the long run, those companies that manage their responsibilities to their shareholders as well as their stakeholders are responsible and well managed and that this is 'good business'.

We can map the possible approaches to CSR considering two variables: profit and public good. CSR can have two possible impacts on each of these variables: it can either increase or reduce profits and can contribute to or harm society and the environment (*The Economist* 2005). Figure 5 shows how four different approaches to CSR can lead to different outcomes on profits and the public good. I label these outcomes bankruptcy, borrowed virtue,[14] bad business and bold business.

Bankruptcy

A company that reduces its profitability and damages the public good does no one any good. It reduces its ability to create and share wealth with its owners, defaulting on its primary obligation. Likewise, by reducing profitability, the ability of the company to reward its employees and create wealth for its suppliers and society is diminished. Even if the reduction in profit is relatively small, the management is in forfeit of their obligations to shareholders and to society. This is especially the case if a company engages in 'CSR' which in fact does harm to society and reduces the public good. This can be through incorrect spending on charitable activities, which reduce the public good in the long run. Some of this spending might be well intentioned, but because companies are inexpert at social spending, it will probably be money wasted.

Official development assistance is full of examples where well-intentioned but ill-conceived and ill-managed projects actually did more harm than good. Donating rice to Nepal, while aiming to improve rural nutrition, reduced the market price and put small farmers out of business — resulting in more poverty. Company contributions to development, especially in disaster relief, sometimes do more harm than good. This usually occurs not because of ill-intent, but because companies are engaging in an activity in which they have no expertise. This is why companies need to stick to their core competences. By moving into fields in which they are not expert, companies risk reducing shareholder returns as well as reducing public good. This risks bankrupting the company, and, if it is done under the guise of CSR, can be seen as morally bankrupt.

Borrowed virtue

Borrowed virtue is when a company spends money on improving the public good in a way which reduces profits. It might appear at first glance that a company that wilfully reduces its profit in order to bring about public good is the very model of corporate social responsibility. In fact it is not. Rather, it is a case of managers indulging their own philanthropic interests, but with someone else's money.

> That is a morally dubious transaction. When Robin Hood stole from the rich to give to the poor, he was still stealing. He might have been a good corporate citizen, but he was still a bandit — and less of one, arguably, than the vicariously charitable CEO, who is spending money taken not from strangers, but from people who have placed him in a position of trust to safeguard their property (*The Economist* 2005).

Of course, if people wish to give their money to an entity that is focused on serving a public good, that is fine. But that is not business. It is philanthropy; it is a private decision and it is to be celebrated — especially if those giving also play an active role in helping make sure the money is well spent (using their personal core competences as entrepreneurs). But when the management of a company decides to reduce their profit by raising public good, they are doing so at someone else's expense. This is why the 'virtue' is borrowed. It still may benefit society, but whether this is the right way for a company to spend investors' money is certainly questionable.

Bad business

Business in the narrow pursuit of self-interest, without concern for the long-term viability of the economy, society and environment, is not sustainable. Even from a purely self-interested perspective, shareholder value is increased by firms that look into the long term and attempt to manage risks. Business that focuses on short-term profits, without accounting for the public good, is bad business in the long run. While in the past it may have been possible, even profitable, to engage in business without concern for the public good, the changing business climate of today means that is no longer tenable. More active civil society monitoring of company activities, greater scientific and public awareness of environmental damage and changing consumer behaviour destines the 'greed is good' approach to business to failure.

It is not in the interests of business to try to avoid their corporate responsibilities. By ignoring environmental problems, the financial impact is simply going to get worse and the cost of clean-up will far exceed the cost of prevention. Equally, the pressing social issues of today are at a point where companies operating in the increasingly globalised world can no longer disclaim responsibility. Even for the compliant corporation, it is in the best interests of shareholders to move towards a proactive CSR policy. But the key is in ensuring that both profit and public good are enhanced through this CSR policy, which requires leadership and vision in order to create the bold business which applies its core competences to the core of its business.

Bold business

To create shared value for shareholders and society, a bold business strategy is required. This is one that seeks to understand what the core competences of the business are, and how these create a unique set of social responsibilities and opportunities. We should be instinctively nervous of CSR policies from companies that all look very much alike, dedicating money to 'worthy causes' without some clarity about how this helps the business. Different companies have very different core competences, and their CSR policies should reflect this.

For instance, Munich Re, the world's second biggest re-insurer, has a core competence in accessing and valuing risks. It has considerable databases of information on weather, seismic, political and other risks which affect businesses. Yet most of the world's businesses, especially in the poor world, do not have access to insurance products that can help them safeguard their futures. This is where Munich Re has led the way on providing knowledge and expertise for micro-insurance, small-scale initiatives (modelled on the micro-finance of the Grameen Bank). In the short term this is an investment of capital and expertise, into helping the worlds poorest manage risk. But it is still an investment in developing future insurance markets and in improving on the company's core competence of accessing and valuing risks, by exposing it to new data sources. This represents a responsible investment of shareholder funds, which makes a solid contribution to society.

Identifying your core competences

Your company's core competence is what makes it special; it is what enables you to compete with and beat the competition; it is what drives profits and helps the business grow. As a management concept it is not new; Prahalad and Hamel discussed it in 1990, and there is little to add to the discussion elsewhere. But the point I wish to make is that your CC should drive your CSR policies and practices. Corporate social responsibility is not a peripheral issue; it should be placed at the heart of the business. I explain in the next section how you can complement your core competences through CSR, but first you need to identify what your core competences are. Prahalad and Hamel (1990) identify three issues that define CC:

- It provides potential access to a wide variety of markets

- It contributes to the benefits of the product as seen by the customer

- It should be difficult for your competitors to imitate

This means that FedEx has a CC in logistics, in managing customer expectations and delivery times across a globalised supply chain. Research in Motion, the makers of BlackBerry email devices, has a core competence in designing user-friendly communication devices. But we need to be careful not to define CC too narrowly. For instance, Nokia, the world's leading mobile phone manufacturer, was right in identifying its CC as being in manufacturing and distributing consumer communication electronics. This enabled Nokia to identify the new market of camera-enabled mobile phones, to recognise that making digital cameras was within its CC and that this presented a new market opportunity. This enabled Nokia to become, by some measures, the world's biggest manufacturer of digital photographic equipment – despite the fact that it never made cameras ten years ago. The CC of Nokia was leveraged to create a new market and head off competition.

When you are identifying your CC, you need to ask yourself the following questions:

- What is the fundamental skill, ability, knowledge, experience, technology or process that got your company to where it is now?

- What is it about your business that makes you unique, different from the competition, and how does this impact on your responsibilities as a corporation?

- Why should staff be proud to work for you and what is special about your staff?

- How can you use these underlying skills, experience and points of difference to use CSR in order to gain competitive advantage?

Once you have started asking yourself these questions, talk with your staff and colleagues and get their opinion. In many cases you will have different ideas initially, but with discussion and debate it should be possible to focus on a couple of key CCs that are important to you and your business. With my consultancy clients I usually ask them to map out their ideas individually. Then as a group they put similar ideas together and give these 'groups' of skills a label as a core competence. We then discuss this, rejecting some and clarifying the existing ideas until the group is comfortable. It is an iterative process that takes time. Identifying core competences is not easy, but it is important. Your CCs are crucial to your business; they should form the basis of your CSR policies and practices, which in turn can create new opportunities for your company.

Complementing your competences with CSR

Once you have established your core competences, it is important to map out the social and environmental issues that affect your business. These can be grouped as general issues, responsibilities and opportunities. General issues are social and environmental issues that concern society but which the company has little effect on and which do not affect its ability to do business. Responsibilities occur wherever the company, through its operations, has an impact — positive or negative. This can include direct environmental impacts, social issues related to doing business and the concerns of stakeholders. Opportunities lie where the company's long-term viability can be influenced, for good or ill, by wider social and environmental issues on which the company has an influence and an interest. Table 1 explains this hierarchy, giving some examples of how these would affect different industries.

What we see from the examples in Table 1 is that different companies, in different industries, face different issues. A FMCG (fast-moving consumer goods) company working in India confronts general issues, outside of its direct control, which are nonetheless crucial to the society in which it operates. The opportunity exists to fulfil its social obligations and grow markets by engaging in fair labour practices and promoting health and sanitation.[15] Whereas the issues that concern the stakeholders (i.e. employees, customers, suppliers) of a European airline are likely to be external — global inequalities and poverty-related disease — the opportunities for the airline lie in focusing on ways in which it can contribute to solving these problems.

While the *general issues* matter, I argue that CSR is not about confronting these problems directly, because the company does not have any expertise in working on these problems. This makes it more likely that the company will reduce both profits and the public good (Bankruptcy, in Figure 5). So, small amounts of cor-

Box 1 **Identifying core competences: an example**

Sometimes it is difficult defining exactly what your core competences are. The solution often takes several steps to arrive at, but understanding your core competences is a useful management tool beyond CSR management. With my clients we walk through a series of stages, trying to understand what makes the company unique. One example is of a medium-sized consultancy firm, which has done very well out of the current metals boom and is eager to 'do some good in the areas where we work'.

Initially the company was donating money to a number of 'worthy charities' without any clear link to its operations. Eager to link its skills with 'doing some good' the company then went through a series of steps to decide on its CCs.

1. A series of staff consultations were held, discussing what causes staff would like to contribute to and how their *specific skills* could be of use to those organisations. These were recorded and analysed

2. Company management were then asked to consider what they thought were the key skills and expertise of the company and these were reviewed against the ideas from the first step

3. A set of ideas, such as: 'helping our clients become more efficient', 'working across borders and language barriers' and 'getting the best out of people' came out of these discussions

4. Distilling these ideas down, the core competences of the company were defined as 'operating globally but understanding local cultures', 'providing the best advisory services for our clients' and 'managing human assets'

5. We then went back to the 'worthy charities' to ask where they would like assistance, using the skills of the company. It turned out that, much more useful than money, these advisory services were of real use to the recipient charities and that staff 'felt good' working with these 'worthy causes', learning more about different areas of the world and reinforcing the company's CCs of 'operating globally but understanding local cultures' and 'managing human assets'

	General issues	Responsibilities	Opportunities
Definition	*Issues that concern society but which the company has little effect on and which do not affect its ability to do business*	*Issues where the company, through its operations, has a direct impact – positive or negative*	*Issues on which the company has an influence where the company's long-term viability can be influenced, for good or ill*
Fast-moving consumer goods company in India	• Poverty and hunger • Curable diseases • Water shortages	• Fair labour practices • Addiction (tobacco) • Local pollution	• Job creation • Urban poverty • Hygiene/sanitation
National European airline	• Global inequalities • AIDS in Africa	• Air pollution • Safety and security	• Climate change • Connecting people
Oil company in Central Asia	• Political problems • Income inequalities • Soviet-era pollution	• Transparency • Rural poverty • Pollution from oil	• Engage with NGOs • Rural infrastructure • Site clean-up

Table 1 **Hierarchy of social and environmental issues**

Source: Adapted from Porter and Kramer 2006

porate philanthropy (as with law firms' pro bono work [Ward 2005]) might be justified in terms of extending a company's licence to operate or for PR impact, but many of these problems are outside of the mandate and competences of CSR.

Where companies need to commit their initial CSR efforts is on addressing their existing responsibilities, discussed below as a form of 'responsive CSR', which is a first step towards corporate social responsibility. But because companies have a long-term obligation to their shareholders, stakeholders, society and the environment, companies also need to be strategic, looking for opportunities to match their core competences with social needs.

Responsive CSR

Responsive CSR is about companies' acknowledging and addressing the responsibilities that they have to their shareholders, stakeholders and society. As a first step this requires compliance with all relevant legislation, but it entails more than just this. A responsible corporation will not engage in corrupt practices, even if they are legal or acceptable in the host country. Most corporate responsibilities, *issues where the company, through its operations, has a direct impact*, will not be voluntary; rather a combination of public pressure and private interest will ensure that companies do take responsibility for the impact of their operations.

Addressing some of these responsibilities requires the modification of the way in which companies conduct business. For textile firms working in poor countries, it is about establishing healthcare schemes and fair labour standards, beyond the bare minimum required by local laws. For FMCG firms, the environmental and social impacts of their products need to be considered and mitigated. The key question is how to go about addressing these responsibilities.

Once the company has identified its core competences and ranked the social and environmental impacts for which it carries a responsibility, the company then needs to analyse response options. This requires the company to identify which responsibilities it has the internal capacity to deal with and which it does not. For an oil company, issues such as rural poverty fall outside of its core competence, so it needs to engage with local communities (discussed in the next chapter). In many cases, however, companies do have core competences which can be leveraged for responsive CSR.

For most responses, to most problems, the company does not need to invent a new solution. In most cases existing technologies, best practices and industry standards can be used and modified to suit the individual case. If water use in a factory is too high, recycling technologies can be used. If transparency in business operations is a problem for an oil company, the Extractive Industries Transparency Initiative can provide answers. The key is for businesses to use their existing capabilities to meet these problems as they arise. In instances when they do not have expertise, and for which a 'standard' solution is not readily available, partnerships are necessary. Matching competences to problems is a good way to minimise the costs of CSR and to ensure that the money that is spent is spent wisely and that it has an impact.

The more effectively companies can leverage their existing core competences and use these to address their responsibilities, at lower costs, the greater benefit they gain over the competition and the greater good they provide to society, creating shared value. But these gains are likely to be temporary, as competitors copy and catch up, thus bold businesses adopt a strategic approach to CSR to help them gain competitive advantage.

Strategic CSR

Strategic CSR is about identifying the *opportunities* that exist for a company. The strategy must be grounded in *issues on which the company has an influence and where the company's long-term viability is at stake* and it must be within the capacity of the company to address these issues. The strategic approach to CSR is about managing risks, growing markets and creating *shared value* for the company and society.

	Core competences	Opportunities	Strategic CSR
Definition	*What makes you special, what enables you to compete with and beat the competition, what drives profits and growth*	*Issues on which the company has an influence where the company's long-term viability can be influenced, for good or ill*	*The company strategy to manage risks, grow markets and create shared value for the company and society*
Munich Re	● Ability to calculate risks and provide insurance products to clients around the world ● Database of weather, seismic, political and other risks	● Global poverty and under-development – increases business risks for Munich Re clients	● Created the Munich Re Foundation to provide knowledge and expertise in micro-insurance. Creating future markets, building Munich Re's CC and promoting economic empowerment
TNT (Netherlands)	● Knowledge of managing fleets, outsourcing, storage locations, system links and transportation ● Maintaining standards and transparency across business units around the world	● Recognition of world hunger as essentially a problem of distribution and logistics, and as a problem that threatens TNT's supply chains and operations	● Strategic partnership between TNT and WFP, providing knowledge transfer (generating savings equivalent to €400,000 annually), technical assistance with HR and transparency initiatives as well as direct assistance in emergency situations

Table 2 **Combining competences and opportunity to create strategic CSR**

> For any company, strategy must go beyond best practices. It is about
> choosing a unique position — doing things differently from com-
> petitors in a way that lowers costs or better serves a particular set of
> customer needs. These principles apply to a company's relation-
> ship to society as readily to its relationship to its customers and
> rivals (Porter and Kramer 2006).

Because of this, there is no single 'right' way to implement CSR strategically in
your business. But the crucial principle is that your core competences need to be
aligned with your CSR strategy, which in turn must be aligned with the opportunities that exist for your business.

Table 2 shows how these can be combined, using examples to explain how this
can work in practice. The Munich Re example has been discussed earlier. The
TNT example is an excellent case of a company leveraging its core competences,
in concert with the World Food Programme (WFP), to make the best use of its
capabilities and to address its corporate responsibilities and opportunities effectively (Murray 2005).

What this table illustrates is how strategic CSR is a culmination of three steps.
First, identifying and ranking the general social issues, corporate responsibilities
and corporate opportunities that exist in your specific business case. Second,
determining your core competences and leveraging these to address your
responsibilities. Third, the strategic aspect is about using your core competences
for your own strategic advantage, creating shared value for your business and
society.

These principles are fine, but the challenge is applying them in your own business. The following case study identifies how the mining company Anglo American went through the process of identifying its core competences, meeting its
responsibilities and then identifying the opportunities for strategic CSR that
existed for the business. Like any real-world examples it is imperfect, there is
always room for improvement (indeed Anglo has constantly evolved its Zimele
programme over the years) and as the competitive environment changes so too
must the strategy for engaging with corporate responsibilities. Yet this case provides guidance on how to integrate strategic CSR into your business, and illustrates the shared value that this can create.

Case study: Anglo American — Zimele

Anglo American is one of the world's largest mining and natural resources companies. Founded in South Africa in 1917, it continues to hold one-third of its assets

in southern Africa, and about two-thirds in developing or transition econo-mies.[16] As a company working in the extractive industries, especially in the developing world, Anglo American faces considerable challenges. First, as an owner of large and mostly immobile assets, the company relies on stable states and regulatory regimes, which requires healthy political societies. Second, the extractive industries have been under − perhaps unparalleled − pressure to deliver development outcomes in the regions in which they operate. Achieving this against a backdrop of HIV/AIDS, worries about the 'resource curse' in coun-tries with high levels of pre-existing poverty, as well as wider sociopolitical prob-lems is a considerable challenge. Third, the rise of 'resource nationalism' has increased the necessity for the extractive industries to gain (and maintain) a 'licence to operate', which goes beyond the traditional permitting arrangements. Put simply: 'your licence to mine is separate from your mining licence' (Nick van Rensberg, Head of Anglo Zimele).

These challenges are considerable, but addressing them responsibly creates opportunities for competitive advantage for firms such as Anglo American which can demonstrate their social contribution to the countries in which they work.

In an effort to confront these challenges in a way that used Anglo American's core competences, the company founded a small business initiative in South Africa in 1989. Named *Zimele* ('to be independent' or 'stand on one's own feet' in Xhosa and Zulu, respectively) this initiative promotes local development by sup-porting the emergence of an entrepreneurial class and creating sustainable local employment. Aimed at integrating local suppliers into the Anglo American sup-ply chain and procurement system, Zimele is founded on a commitment of cre-ating value for society through employment, while also constituting a responsi-ble investment of Anglo American's finance and expertise. Anglo Zimele is not charity, as Jonathan Samuel, International Social and Community Development Manager notes: 'Zimele is not a part of our social investment programme − rather it is responsible execution of core business'.[17]

This core business approach is one that also creates 'shared value', an outcome that has been recognised as the programme continues to expand with more investment from the company and with new enterprise development models being deployed, such as the Anglo Khula Mining Fund and new Enterprise Development Hubs. Although lessons have been learned along the way, Anglo Zimele is a useful example of how high-level corporate commitment can be matched by local action, to create value for society. This in turn has helped the company confront some of the challenges it faces operating in difficult environ-ments, securing shareholder value in the long run.

Corporate challenges

The extractive industries have not always acted responsibly in the past; nor does the industry as a whole enjoy a positive reputation today. Moreover, the locations in which most extractive firms operate tend to suffer from poor governance and weak democratic institutions. Operating within this environment is not in the interests of business. This is why leading companies such as Anglo American have made a *strategic business decision* to confront the challenges they face, by working in partnership with local governments, NGOs and development agencies. Here it is important to recognise that weak and corrupt governments, poor and unhealthy communities and HIV/AIDS are *shared problems* that require *common solutions*. Companies have a role to play, but this needs to be implemented in concert with government and international initiatives. Before discussing how these can be addressed by businesses through CSR, it is important to understand a little more about these problems and how they affect companies such as Anglo American.

Fixed assets: fluid politics

Almost all of the assets that Anglo American owns are fixed – they cannot easily be moved and rely on stable local conditions to operate. Mines, mills and processing plants are large and immobile assets that need healthy and well-trained workforces to operate. Mines are, in a sense, very expensive holes in the ground, which cannot be moved. Further, two-thirds of Anglo American's assets are located in developing and transition economies where standards of governance, education, healthcare and infrastructure are often low. Many of these developing countries suffer, to varying degrees, from high levels of corruption. Moreover, the 'resource curse' (discussed next) is frequently associated with the extractive industries working in the developing world. This poses a considerable challenge for mining companies, as Anglo American's CEO explained:

> Some people might imagine that a major mining company would find it convenient to work in places where there are weak governments. This could not be further from the truth. We welcome regulatory certainty and we like operating where there are strong regulatory frameworks that command public confidence. Ultimately our operations stand or fall on the basis of trust. We work hard to build trust but it is much better if, in addition to our efforts, communities feel that their government looks after their interests and ensures accountability. It is much more difficult for us to achieve good development outcomes where there is poor governance (Carrol 2007).

In developed countries, with strong states, companies can be confident that in paying their taxes they are contributing to the country's education, healthcare and infrastructure. But in many developing countries this cannot be taken for granted. Corruption, the misuse of public office and funds for private gain, undermines this link. In the long run companies find it more difficult, indeed more expensive, to operate in corrupt countries.

Moreover, their ability to seek new exploration and production opportunities is based on the ability to gain trust; engagement with corrupt regimes undermines this. The Extractive Industries Transparency Initiative (EITI) was established as a multi-government, industry and NGO partnership to encourage greater accountability and debate, based on the principle of 'publish what you pay'. This is a useful initiative in which many companies are now engaged. But the responsibilities, and opportunities, for the extractive industries also extend to being a partner in creating sustainable development.

Creating sustainable development

The extractive industries have come under considerable pressure – from host governments, NGOs, activist shareholders and others – to contribute to sustainable development. In South Africa this pressure is acute; communities and the government expect companies to deliver development to the regions in which they operate.[18] In particular the legal requirements for Black Economic Empowerment (BEE) in all company's operations, as well as specific requirements established in the Mining Charter, require mining houses to *demonstrate how they are creating sustainable development.*

While companies are not development agencies, they are actors in the development process. Besides paying their taxes – and making sure that these tax revenues are reported and properly used – companies also need to create value for their staff, stakeholders and society. This pressure to contribute to sustainable development is heightened in countries such as South Africa where HIV/AIDS, worries over the 'resource curse' and wider social issues have come to the fore.

The spread of HIV/AIDS undermines development, weakens the supply of workers and threatens the very viability of some communities in southern Africa. Checking the spread of HIV/AIDS through antiretroviral drugs is essential for both companies and society. The private sector, in partnership with governments and the international community, needs to be part of the solution.

In 2002 Anglo American was the first major employer in Africa, indeed in the world, to provide free antiretroviral treatment to all of its HIV-positive employees, starting a programme that now covers over 15,000 workers. The positive impact that this has on communities and the wider society is considerable, a fact acknowledged by the Government of South Africa. This US$10 million a year investment in creating value for society is also paying off for the company through reduced absenteeism and fewer skilled workers lost to the disease. This is why Anglo American's International Social and Community Development Manager, Jonathan Samuel, sees the HIV programme 'as part of our core business, in providing healthcare for our employees'.[19]

It is important for companies to address these country- or region-wide issues, as well as concerns specific to their own operations as part of their CSR programme. Problems unique to the mining sector — such as advance planning on how eventual mine closures will impact local communities — need to be addressed. Equally, wider issues of economic development — including disadvantaged and minority groups — is increasingly on the agenda for the extractive industries. This is especially true when discussing the resource curse.

The resource curse, or paradox of plenty, is the theory that those countries with the most natural resources tend to have lower economic growth than others (Auty 1993). Driven by poor governance and underinvestment in social and human capital, as well as broad economic impacts such as the 'Dutch Disease' that can impact on wealthy and well-run countries, the resource curse has in the past deprived many nations and communities of the development they deserve. But this need not be the case. Many states have done extremely well out of resource extraction — such as South Africa, Chile, Brazil, Australia and Canada — achieving this by diversifying away from natural resources to an extent that they are no longer deemed to be natural-resource-dependent. These success stories have also demonstrated the importance of good governance as a precondition for avoiding the 'resource curse'.[20]

This is why in helping to create sustainable development and avoid the resource curse, the extractive industries need to find ways to replace the natural capital they extract from countries with human, social and financial capital — which remains after the natural resource has been extracted. Demonstrating how companies are creating this value for society helps to build their 'licence to operate' which is essential in an era of growing resource nationalism.

Resource nationalism and a licence to operate

The culmination of concerns about the resource curse, companies extracting assets without returning value to society and a distrust of global capitalism has led to an increase in 'resource nationalism'. This has seen countries taking an increasingly isolationist or nationalist approach to extracting their natural resources. This makes it difficult for companies such as Anglo American to sustain its resource base. The rising tide of resource nationalism is making it even more important that companies earn their 'licence to operate'. For those companies that can demonstrate a willingness and ability to create value for society, this can be a source of competitive advantage – based on an enhanced licence to operate.

This licence is more than official permitting. The licence to operate means having the support of local communities (including indigenous communities in places such as Australia and Canada), having legitimacy with local governments and ultimately being trusted by stakeholders to conduct operations in a way that creates value for society and safeguards the environment. Gaining this licence to operate is essential: to prevent the threat to resource nationalism, reduce the risk of shutdowns due to local dissatisfaction and ultimately to protect the value of the company. But doing it well is a considerable challenge, as well as an opportunity, as the Anglo Zimele initiative shows.

Zimele: 'To be independent', to 'stand on one's own feet'

In 1989, before the downfall of apartheid, Anglo American established a small business initiative, Zimele, to create local opportunities and contribute to social and economic development. Based on a decision from the very top of Anglo American, and a corporate history of opposing apartheid including initiatives dating back to the 1950s, Zimele was established to help the company create value for the communities in which it works. The founding objectives were to:

- Create access to mainstream business opportunities for historically disadvantaged South Africans

- Create sustainable, commercially viable, enterprises driven by people with passion and entrepreneurial spirit

- Contribute to the sustainable development of mining communities

The Zimele concept is based on using the company's core competences to help local entrepreneurs contribute to – and benefit from – the company's supply chain and procurement. Anglo American contributes its core competences to start-up businesses and procurement partners, aiming to create diversified (not dependent) enterprises. This benefits the company directly through having a more flexible and robust supply chain, and indirectly by developing a competitive advantage based on the company's ability to create value for society while maintaining profitability.

Which core competences?

Anglo American, as a global mining and natural resources company, has core competences in several key areas. First it has core business and *commercial* skills, knowledge of how to operate business units and ensure internal governance and accountability. Second, it has specific *technical* expertise in mining and resource extraction and an ability to translate this technical knowledge into practical outcomes. Third, it has access to considerable *finance* and the acumen to employ this capital profitably.

These core competences form the basis of Anglo American's operations as a global firm. Translating these core competences into useful tools for community development relied on identifying areas where these skills were lacking and discerning how they could be usefully employed. Anglo American identified that the supply chain and procurement process in South Africa was one such opportunity. This is a huge opportunity, as demonstrated by looking at the company's outgoing payments in 2006, as shown in Figure 6, which illustrates company-wide financial outgoings.

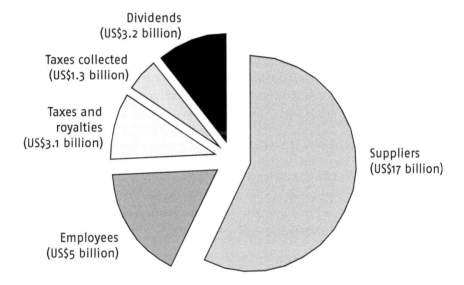

Figure 6 **Anglo American plc financial outgoings: suppliers and shareholders**

Because of a lack of local suppliers, Anglo's South African business units were purchasing most of their supplies from distant suppliers, adding to the cost and reducing flexibility. At the same time, unemployment and poverty were big issues in the mining areas, the impacts of which created business risks for mining operations. Identifying that the lack of local suppliers was due, at least in part, to a lack of entrepreneurial expertise, a limited technical knowledge and a paucity of finance, a clear *opportunity* existed for Anglo American. The company decided to try to create value for society and shareholders by encouraging local business development, through supply chain development.

Anglo Zimele business model

The Anglo Zimele business model is based on developing businesses and assisting them in accessing procurement opportunities. It is a 'hard business' solution that expects partners to engage in risk sharing and to move quickly, within three years, towards independence from the programme. Anglo Zimele purchases minority stakes (10–30%) in partner companies, as well as making loans available on broadly commercial terms. These loans are leveraged using the Anglo American name, thus securing much cheaper credit than would otherwise be available, and finance is available to BEE partners to assist them in buying their share of the equity. This is a case of leveraging the company's core competence of finance and contributing it to companies that normally cannot access credit. These financial risks are balanced by ensuring that all Anglo Zimele companies adhere to the Anglo Business Principles – which govern issues such as internal accountability, transparency and corruption – thus leveraging another of Anglo American's core competences in a way that benefits both the small enterprise and Anglo Zimele.

In exchange for equity, Anglo Zimele gains representation on the board of the company. This enables Anglo Zimele 'business development officers' to provide targeted assistance that is useful and relevant to the company. This commercial expertise and technical input is the contribution deemed most useful by partner companies. For example, Steve Mnguni of Thabo Piping Systems explained that:

> Partnering with Zimele enabled a big step for me ... I know all about the pipe business but I needed training and skills to go into business, now I am looking at using these business skills in growing another business for trucks and delivery.[21]

The training and expertise provided to each firm depends on its needs, but essential services such as tax information, providing minutes for board meetings and company secretary tasks are provided for free by Zimele by a team of in-house experts. 'The company secretary work is very helpful, that is something that none of us are any good at. The secretarial, corporate governance side, that is good, it is really needed' (Kit Manley, Head of Calulo Drilling).[22]

In addition Zimele companies gain a certain level of 'free' access to Anglo Technical Division (the company's in-house technical support division), to management and accountancy training as well as to support in implementing health and safety standards.[23] It is because the Zimele business model is deliberately private-sector-focused that Anglo American is also able to leverage its core competence as a commercial organisation, providing business planning and corporate governance support to create viable businesses.

> We take a 'tough love' approach ... you don't help create entrepreneurs by being soft, so we run Anglo Zimele on broadly economic

terms. But what makes it different is the mentoring we provide. This meets the needs of the enterprise: for example, corporate governance, accounting, operating in markets, safety and sustainable development. The support is targeted at the needs of each enterprise (Edward Bickham, Executive Vice President − External Affairs).[24]

For existing small-scale suppliers, Anglo Zimele works with divisional supply chain personnel to identify local procurement opportunities. The focus here is on helping BEE suppliers to access the opportunities of participating in a larger procurement network. These procurement partnerships are built on clear commercial principles of quality, price, service and delivery, and cost savings.

Ideally these 'first contracts' for new companies can then be used to grow a viable, independent business. For instance Coal Fields Panel Beaters, a joint venture between Zimele (holding 20% equity), a BEE entrepreneur and another partner (both holding 40% equity) started business by successfully tendering for panel beating work with several Anglo coal mines. However access to credit, financial training and the essential 'first contract' has enabled Coal Fields to grow and gain work with insurance companies and private clients. These insurance contracts now eclipse the Anglo coal contracts, but, in the words of BEE partner Simon Ngubuni: 'To get the work with the insurance companies − they need to know us. This is where having the Zimele 'stamp' helped us, so now we are really a growing business'.[25]

Thus the key contribution of Anglo Zimele is one of *facilitation*, not charity. This facilitation is aimed at providing mentoring and support to enable BEE suppliers to contribute tenders and comply with Anglo American procurement standards, but it does not guarantee that they will win these tenders.

> What we don't do is say to firms, 'this is the price to quote to win the tender'. Instead we help them to access tender documents, make sure they know how to tender properly and explain what this all means. We are still driven by price and quality in making business decisions (Edward Bickham, Executive Vice President − External Affairs). [26]

This support for integration into the Anglo American supply chain is balanced by also encouraging firms to diversify their supply to other businesses, in an effort to avoid dependence. Indeed, business development officers consider it a success if companies grow to a stage where they are fully independent: 'We are always looking for an exit strategy, on how we can reinvest our money in new opportunities. These companies should be able to succeed without us once we are gone' (Louwrens de Jager, Business Development Officer − Anglo Zimele).

Because of these returns, and fresh injections of capital from the company, the Anglo Zimele fund has expanded considerably over the past years with considerable new funding set to be added in 2008. The company continues to provide core funding to pay for the operational and infrastructure costs of Anglo Zimele. This is seen as a worthwhile investment that pays dividends both in terms of creating value for society and in helping Anglo American build a competitive advantage as a firm that delivers on its social commitments.

Competitive advantage?

> We don't do this to create a competitive advantage, we do it because it is the right thing to do – if we also gain that is fine – but we do it to help in the communities in which we work. We do it because it is the right thing to do (Godfrey Gomwe, Chairman of Anglo Zimele).[27]

Creating value for society and returning dividends to communities is essential for Anglo American's continued operations. The question is whether Anglo Zimele also creates value and enhances returns for shareholders. To examine this, we need to look for ways in which Anglo American's Zimele (and other social programmes) create *shared value* by giving the company a competitive advantage. That is, how does creating value for society assist the company to outperform its competitors?

Turning back to the three main challenges faced by Anglo American in its global operations: political risks and fixed assets, the pressure to deliver sustainable development and the rise in resource nationalism. We see that the Anglo Zimele programme does help to overcome some of the challenges of working in the developing world by enhancing its licence to operate. This is achieved by demonstrating that the company is returning value to the community and society. This enhanced licence to operate enables Anglo American to continue to work and, because of its position as a responsible operator, to access new areas and resources based on its 'social capital' (Jones *et al.* 2007).

This enhanced licence to operate is achieved in several ways. First, by assisting the company to meet its BEE targets, as set by the government in the Mining Charter, Anglo American demonstrates compliance with the statutory requirements of South Africa. Moreover, Anglo Zimele has been recognised by the President, Thabo Mbeki, as a leader in demonstrating how BEE can produce a vibrant and viable class of 'previously disadvantaged' entrepreneurs. This assists the company in bidding for new development areas within South Africa, as an established 'responsible' actor that goes beyond legal minimums and basic compliance.

Second, the company benefits from having access to a local supply chain, providing greater flexibility and cost savings. Aside from the benefits of having a locally available supply chain, the company also gains from engagement with small-scale entrepreneurs. The belief demonstrated here is that exposing executives to the challenges faced in starting new businesses is inherently good for staff development, helping to build an entrepreneurial culture *within* Anglo American. For instance, one individual is currently working within Zimele for 18 months as part of his training in the Anglo American Graduate Development Programme.

Third, perhaps most importantly but most difficult to demonstrate, gaining access to new resources increasingly relies on gaining the licence to operate in difficult social and environmental conditions. Having a proven 'test case' of how the company has been able to deliver value for society has been used by the company when bidding for new projects in Peru, Alaska and Chile (where the Anglo Zimele model has recently been introduced, alongside a micro-credit facility). Indeed, the Chile programme won a 'Presidential Seal' in 2008, one of just seven awarded across Chile to celebrate the country's bicentenary in 2010, illustrating the political support that these initiatives help to deliver. Although these projects were decided primarily on the basis of price and highest bidder, the company believes that in the long term their enterprise development initiatives will create competitive advantage.

As societies and vibrant democracies expect more from the extractive industries, companies such as Anglo American, which can demonstrate an ability to create value for society, gain a competitive advantage. This is why the Anglo Zimele case is a good example of how creating value for society can also create shareholder value, by using the company's core competences for the public good.

Conclusions

Corporate social responsibility is not about charity and international companies are not development agencies. But companies can be agents of development – as the Anglo Zimele case demonstrates. Although financing is important for small-scale business development, companies can make an even greater contribution by using their core competences for CSR. This in turn creates value for the company: directly through improving the local supply chain and enhancing the licence to operate, as well as indirectly, through the benefits of working in a healthy and prosperous society.

The lesson from Anglo Zimele is that opportunities do exist for companies to create shared value. Sometimes this will involve taking difficult decisions; the solution may not always be obvious. But, by using your company's core competences to create value for society, opportunities exist to also enhance shareholder value. There is no single solution on *what* to do; each industry and each company has a different set of challenges to face. *How* companies use their core competences to create shared value can, however, create competitive advantage and will increasingly define corporations and their relationship to society. As with any business decision, the challenge is to outperform the competition and to innovate to create new solutions to previously intractable problems. In doing this you should leverage – indeed enhance – your company's core competences to create shared value.

3

Collaborate based on common values

Discovering the value of collaboration with communities and other stakeholders is essential for implementing CSR and creating shared value. There are plenty of areas where businesses are not expert, where complex problems cannot be solved alone, which is where collaboration with external partners is needed. This is why it is crucial that you partner with the right organisations and in the right way. This collaboration needs to be built on *common values*, shared understandings of how to define the problems and how to arrive at solutions. By bringing together the diverse capabilities of partners, these common values can then be used to create shared value.

Implementing CSR is best achieved by harnessing the strengths of other organisations when leveraging your own core competences. Achieving this requires effective partnerships. Collaboration can bring together the core competences of your business while accessing the core competences of your partners, to achieve together what would have been impossible alone.

Each partner needs to gain something of value from the partnership. For your business this primarily needs to be profit, greater returns to shareholders, especially in the long run. But this should be done in a way that also enhances the returns to stakeholders, creates value for society and helps protect the environment. But it is important to acknowledge that different partners will have their own hierarchy of interests. NGOs will have a focus primarily on meeting the needs of their stakeholders — they have no shareholders as such to return a profit to. Governments, working with businesses, have their own agendas and responsibilities which they must meet. It is crucial that you understand these different interests, find common values and interests on which to agree, and create shared value from this collaboration. This point is illustrated by the Montana Exploradora and AMAC case study later in this chapter.

Collaboration can take different forms. Public–private partnerships, multistakeholder initiatives, ad hoc collaboration and contracting are all possible. The exact form your collaboration takes is something that needs to be considered strategically to fit your individual business case. It should be needs-driven. What this should not be is 'cookie-cutter' CSR, identical across business cases and limited in impact. Rather, strategic CSR is built on long-term relationships that address the interests and capacities of each side. Depending on the business risks and opportunities developed in Chapter 2, you need to identify your business needs. These strategic interests, and opportunities for value creation, should be matched to partners that share both the common values and the capacity to create shared value.

Different partners bring different competences and priorities to your CSR strategy. NGOs and local communities can contribute new skills, ideas and legitimacy. They can also obstruct progress by an unwillingness to take risks or by focusing on their own narrow agenda (see Chapter 7). The key to getting the best out of collaboration with NGOs, UN agencies, governments and communities is in defining these partnerships in a way that is in the long-term interests of all parties. A risk management strategy is also needed to ensure that value creation is in the interests of all parties. Implementing these partnerships requires a clear set of objectives from both parties and a plan on how to realise this goal.

For corporations, especially those in the extractive industries, building partnerships can provide legitimacy and enhance the 'licence to operate'. On the other hand, for the UN or for NGOs wishing to operate in areas where they have little sway with governments, 'the economic power of large corporates can be a useful influence . . . [e.g.] helping refugees in a country that had not signed up to an international treaty' (Findlay 2007).

The Montana Exploradora and AMAC case study at the end of this chapter shows how it is possible for a company to use strategic community relationships to implement a strategic CSR agenda. This has helped to create value for society and aided in environmental protection — in a way that would have been impossible working alone. The Montana and AMAC case also shows how it is possible to define strategic *business* objectives and to use strategic CSR as a tool to enhance shareholder returns, while also enhancing stakeholder, social and environmental impacts. These solutions could not have been created by the company (or governments, communities or NGOs) alone. Collective action was required to create shared value for all parties. But experience also teaches us that creating these sorts of 'win–win' solution requires a clear understanding of your goals and a well-defined strategy for achieving these.

Creating shared value through common values

The objective of strategic CSR is to enhance shareholder returns, while improving the social and environmental performance of your business. This in turn drives future profits, further increasing shareholder value and enabling the company to continue creating stakeholder value. This *shared value* approach is one where societal goals and shareholder objectives meet. Creating shared value in an enduring fashion relies on the power of partnerships. Of course there are limitations to collaboration, limitations that are well set out by David Vogel in his 2006 book *The Market for Virtue: The Potential and Limits of Corporate Social Responsibility*. Companies are not inherently good at working with non-corporate partners and many NGOs struggle to deliver results that are understandable to their corporate collaborators.

This is why strategic relationships need to be extended beyond the typical understanding of alliances between two businesses to work together, towards collaboration with NGOs, communities, governments and society. These strategic relationships need to go beyond just giving money to charity and should not be based on a simple profit motive. Corporate charity is the sort of 'borrowed virtue' discussed in Chapter 2, which improves the public good (although not nearly as much as if expertise and core competence is contributed) at the expense of shareholders. Likewise, the 'bad business' approach of increasing profits at the expense of society and the environment is neither desirable nor sustainable. This is where 'bold business' is required, which seeks to increase shareholder returns as well as the public good.

It cannot be stressed enough that companies and NGOs, when pursuing partnerships, need to be explicit in planning how the collaboration will work (Stott 2007). They must also identify early on any risks and potential problems. Not all corporate values and stakeholder interests will be aligned, so it is necessary to specify the limits of the partnership. In setting out how this collaboration will work it is crucial to plan for possible negative outcomes but you should also avoid the 'cookie-cutter' approach of unoriginal CSR solutions.

Cookie-cutter CSR

Too often when we see companies talking about their CSR policies, detailing their 'good works' in their annual report, it is all very much the same. The company makes a bold-sounding statement about how it is 'committed to sustainability' and that it 'recognises its responsibilities to society and the environment'. This is then followed by a series of disconnected examples of how some of its business units have improved – for example, energy efficiency – without any group-wide or company-wide analysis. Then this sort of cookie-cutter CSR report tends to finish by discussing the contributions a company makes to charity, which tend to sound large, but in reality are quite small.

Sadly, this cookie-cutter CSR is all too common in the corporate world, risking making the same mistakes of the 'greenwash' reports of the 1980s. Perhaps more importantly, cookie-cutter CSR does not make a real or lasting contribution to society and the environment, nor does it enhance shareholder returns. This is because companies are contributing their cash but not their core competences to addressing social and environmental problems. If we are to confront the major challenges of our time – climate change, regional inequalities, poverty, AIDS and other diseases – then more than charitable giving is required. If companies are to manage their risks and invest in long-term sustainability, charitable giving is not the solution. An *investment* in sustainability is needed.

Also, there are some very real questions about whether companies should be engaged in issues that do not meet with either their social impacts/risks, or their capacities to address these. While companies are part of wider society and need to contribute to broad social issues, such as global poverty, this is what taxes are for. Governments exist to confront these wider issues. It is only when companies are affecting, or are affected by, particular issues that they need to get involved. When they do, companies need to take their responsibilities seriously and address these issues in a strategic manner.

But when these wider issues are left to companies to address, then some real questions need to be asked about the 'democratic deficit' that this encourages. Companies are not accountable to the wider public to the same extent that governments are – so we should be careful in transferring too much responsibility (and through this power and influence) – to companies that continue to exist to serve their owners. While companies should be engaged in social and environmental problems, many of the answers lie outside of the business world, while much of the finance and capabilities exist within companies. Companies are not *development agencies* but they can be effective *agents of development*. This is why engagement from businesses, as well as governments and NGOs, is essential. To do this, collaboration, not charitable giving, is the right approach.

What do your partners value?

The first step in building collaborations is finding the right people and groups to collaborate with. To do this you need to understand the different core competences of your potential partners, what it is that they value, and from this the strategic relationship opportunities. Given that your business probably already has some form of CSR policy, or even ad hoc collaboration with charities and local governments, these existing relationships can form the basis of your strategic CSR plan. Trust probably exists with these organisations and this is a crucial component of any relationship.

What is essential is redefining the collaboration in terms of creating shared value. Table 3 provides a simple way in which you can work through the steps of identifying what potential partners value, how this fits with their core competences and from this the strategic partnership opportunities that exist. To make the lessons practical the table uses a hypothetical example of a company operating a gold mine in a European country.

What we see in the example given in Table 3 is that there are clear opportunities for collaboration. For example, in localising the supply chain of certain products both to reduce corporate costs and to improve local job creation, an *opportunity* exists to meet local government concerns at the same time as improving shareholder value. The core competences of each of the partners can be used, in very different ways, to work towards a common goal.

Likewise, the gold mine values a predictable business climate, with clear and achievable environmental regulations, resulting in reduced likelihood of a costly mine shutdown. This kind of 'flexible regulation', as discussed in Chapter 6, can help the company to manage its risks while ensuring local environmental protection. There are, however, some issues, such as global environmental problems, which the company is not contributing to (nor can it substantively improve) which matter a great deal to the environmental NGO. This is where the partners need to be clear that, while they are collaborating on local environmental issues, their shared value does not extend to, for example, global climate change. Some local initiatives could be promoted, including reporting by the company to support awareness-raising activities, but any partnership should be limited to the areas where opportunities exist for shared value creation.

Having identified the ways in which different partners can create value from collaboration, this needs to be put into practice. It is important at this point to begin to look at the values and beliefs that you have in common with different partners. As noted earlier, trust is crucial to this. If you think through any of your existing business relationships, trust undoubtedly plays a big role. In engaging with non-business partners, the expectations and modes of working are different, the risks the higher — so trust is even more important.

	Core competences	What they value	Strategic partnership opportunities
Definition	*The key skills, capacities and commitments of the organisation that enable it to achieve its goals better than others can*	*Issues that are central to the organisation and that define its purpose (legitimacy) and mode of operations*	*How the organisation's capacities can be leveraged to improve what it values, in ways not possible working alone*
Private company: 'responsible mining'	● Ability to manage financial investments and risks in a way that maximises mine output ● Experience in innovating operations to meet environmental regulations	● Wealth creation for shareholders ● Ensuring consistent and predictable mine outputs without shutdowns	● Invest in local businesses to reduce supply chain costs and build the local economy ● Improve environmental benchmarking to ensure no mine shutdowns
Local government	● Community contacts and involvement of neighbourhood networks in local government and consultation ● Legitimacy in dealing with resource management and environmental issues	● Local economic development and job creation ● Preserving the local environment for current and future generations	● Mobilise community networks to help build local businesses, possibility of joint funding ● Collaborative and flexible regulation of the environment
Environ-mental NGO	● Mobilisation of individuals, school groups and civil society on specific issues ● Education and awareness of small groups: leads to legitimacy and respect	● Healthy lifestyles and a healthy local environment ● Global environmental issues and concerns	● Work with local networks and groups to promote local development and job creation ● Promote local initiatives to reduce the environmental impact

Table 3 **Identifying value creation opportunities for a gold mine**

Box 2 **Thought provoker: Chinese contracts**

Charles Handy, in describing a negotiation he had as a young manager for an oil company, explained how he came to rethink negotiation and contracts. His experience of reaching an agreement with a Chinese trader who then refused to sign any documents caused him to reflect on the use of legal contracts to enforce agreements. His reflection was that mutually beneficial deals, partnerships, were likely to be much more durable than legal agreements:

> The Chinese Contract . . . was about the importance of compromise as a prerequisite for progress. Both sides have to concede for both to win. It was about the need for trust and a belief in the future. Writ large, it was about sacrifice, the willingness to forego some present good to ward off future evil, or, more positively, it was about investment – spending now in order to gain later (Handy 1995).

Although he was talking about business contracts, in Box 2 Charles Handy seems to be discussing CSR well before it was popularised. The concept of making sacrifices in order to avoid future problems, of seeing this as a strategic investment in the future, fits well with the idea of strategic CSR. Applying this lesson to collaboration, it is more important to determine the opportunities for creating shared value. When both partners have a stake in the success of the project, it is much more likely to succeed. But to ensure that shared value can be created, the partners need to be working from a set of common values that define their work.

Defining common values

Shared value is about creating wealth and opportunities, fulfilling concrete goals and objectives for partners in corporate social responsibility. But these partnerships need to be built on more than just short-term interests. There must be common values, shared beliefs and commitments to issues that concern both parties. A partnership between a polluter and an environmental NGO will only work if both parties have shared ideals, a common vision of reducing pollution and improving economic growth. An anti-business NGO, or a company that is simply not interested in environmental protection, will not be able to sustain a relationship. If you are building new collaborations for your CSR agenda, or if you are reviewing your existing collaborations, you need to ask yourself the following questions:

- Why are we engaged in CSR?

- How does CSR spending and investment affect our business?

- Will we still be spending money on CSR during the next budget cut?

- If we weren't funding this NGO's work, would they still be doing it?

- If it weren't for the PR impact, why would we fund this charity?

- What is the ultimate goal of our CSR programme?

These questions help to clarify, both for yourself and for your partners, exactly what your shared values are. This is also where having external assistance, a CSR adviser who can listen to your staff, suppliers, stakeholders and potential partners and help you better understand what these common values are, is of great help. A good CSR adviser will help you begin to understand what values — corporate and personal — you hold as important and then how you can build strategic partnerships with those organisations that share some of those values.

Collaboration is only an appropriate approach when goals, motives and value systems are compatible. Different partners should be linked through trust relationships and must understand each other — agreeing on the common goal and having a common understanding of how each side will contribute to achieving this goal. In short 'Partners need to be committed to finding common ground for a partnership to work' (Findlay 2007).

Strategic collaboration opportunities

Once you have been through the three steps above, you should have identified:

- How the core competences of your company can be leveraged, along with other organisations, to create shared value that would be impossible alone

- What value can be created for your company, and for your potential partners, through collaboration and how this will drive the relationship forwards

- Which corporate values, beliefs and goals, you have in common with potential partners and understand how these will help sustain the collaboration

At this point you can then begin to look for partnership opportunities that contribute to your CSR strategy. This *strategic* approach to CSR relies on all project partners having a common interest in success, a common understanding of what these successes will be and a common desire to achieve these goals collectively. Choosing the right strategic partners is one of the most important decisions that you will make in implementing your CSR strategy. With the right partners, working in unison to create shared value, and sustained by common values, your company can improve profits and the public good. Carrying this objective through into practice is still not easy, no matter how good your partners are, which is why you need to adopt a partnership plan.

Charting towards collaboration

How you structure your strategic collaboration will be determined by a number of factors. The level of financial commitment, the extent of overlap with your core business functions, who your partners are and the levels of risk involved for each party will all determine exactly how you chart your way towards collaboration. The key point to consider is that the collaboration should reflect the rest of your business model, allowing you to leverage your core competence. As with any business decision, there is no 'right' model for how to partner with other organisations. With any attempt to set a 'model' for partnership, there is a risk of a 'cookie-cutter' CSR policy, removing the innovation and competition that presents the greatest *opportunities* in CSR work. That said, the people you will be partnering with are not the same as the people you make most other business decisions with.

Partnering with NGOs, who have very different ideas of value creation and possibly quite different values from businesses, can be a challenge. This is why I explain in this chapter the particular issues to be aware of when partnering with NGOs, some of the pitfalls and the importance of building personal relationships with your counterparts. Likewise, entering into public–private partnerships (PPPs) has become very popular, so I provide some guidance here on the specific issues and opportunities of this sort of partnership in its broader sense. Perhaps most importantly, whatever form your partnership takes, the issue of risk sharing needs to be managed properly.

NGOs

'Non-governmental organisations' is a very broad term, encompassing a wide range of groups. NGOs range from the very small to the very big, from local to global, from constructive to obstructive, from excellent partners to liabilities. These NGOs are all part of 'civil society', the innocuous group that is not governmental and is not for profit (which is not to say that some do not make a profit).

In part this is made much more difficult by the growth in the number of NGOs in the past few years. It is estimated that there are over 50,000 international NGOs operating today (2008); national NGOs are even more numerous. There are over 2 million NGOs operating in the United States and in India — where 75% have one or fewer full-time paid staff.[28] The growth in 'not-for-profit consultancies' and other 'NGOs' that take advantage of tax benefits raises questions about exactly who and what constitutes an NGO. In fact some observers cynically note that NGOs can become a job creation vehicle for their founders, accountable only to their donors — not to those they claim to help (Roy 2004).

One of my most enduring memories of NGOs was in Pakistan. At the time the government was making NGO registration much more difficult; some NGOs had been used as cover for Islamist or anti-President Musharraf activities and there was considerable pressure on international donors to intervene. I asked one of our counterparts, the head of a local NGO, what his biggest challenge was in his work. He replied: 'The Lahore Stock exchange won't allow me to list; is this something you can help me with?'

Of course this is an extreme example; there are some excellent NGOs that do outstanding and selfless work. Because of the tremendous number of NGOs one must be very careful in making broad statements. But it is fair to say, as I explain in Chapter 7, that many NGOs lack the very transparency, legitimacy and accountability that they argue governments and businesses are deficient in. This is why it is crucial that you 'know' your NGO partners, in much the same way as you 'know' your customers and 'know' your normal business partners.

If you enter into partnership with an NGO you are taking a business risk and it is crucial that you know as much as possible about your potential partner. This is where holding common values is crucial, which is why personal relationships need to form the core of your partnership with the NGO community. Partnering with the right NGO can be a key part of your strategic CSR policy, but it is vital that you choose the right partner and that this partnership is based on personal and professional trust. As with any business partnership, starting with small-scale collaboration, conducting adequate due diligence and assessing the risks in advance are all crucial. But, as with all business decisions, sometimes taking a risk produces a large return. You should not be afraid of partnering with a small, innovative NGO over a large, bureaucratic one if there are shared values and a common understanding of what you both hope to achieve.

PPPs

Collaboration with governments can take many forms. The sort of local government partnership that was discussed earlier in this chapter is one example of the sorts of innovative CSR opportunities that exist. Working with government officials, finding what they value and creating opportunities for collaboration, is a common issue. In Chapter 6 these topics are discussed in depth, detailing how businesses need to adapt their practices in order to work with governments. One particular form of partnership opportunity, which has certainly grown in popularity recently, is public–private partnerships (PPPs).

Public–private partnerships are, in a narrow sense, agreements between the state and companies to provide specific goods and services over a defined time span.[29] Examples include managing municipal water supplies, large infrastructure investments and private provision of state services (jails, roads, etc.).[30] In these PPPs the private sector uses its core competences of financing, greater efficiency and lower costs of distribution, and the public sector ensures universal access by providing financial support and subsidies: 'Thereby enabling private firms to enter large markets with guaranteed consumers' (UN Millennium Project 2006).

This definition has widened now to include informal PPP arrangements and wider-level engagements such as the Global Compact.[31] These are aimed at addressing broad social and environmental issues such as climate change, public health and persistent poverty. The benefit of these partnerships is that they leverage not only finance but also business expertise. This is the key point of PPPs: they seek to combine the respective strengths of the private and public sectors, creating win–win solutions. This broadening definition was stated by the World Economic Forum as involving:

> Business and/or not-for-profit civil society organizations working in partnership with government agencies, including official development institutions. It entails reciprocal obligations and mutual accountability, voluntary or contractual relationships, the sharing of investment and reputational risks, and joint responsibility for design and execution (WEF 2005).

This is where partnership is about *process*, of a way in which businesses and governments choose to work together rather than separately, when confronting challenges that are too big or too complex to be managed separately. In some cases business needs to take the lead. For instance, we have seen in 2007 that it is the corporate community, in concert with specific states (California, New Hampshire), that has shown the lead on carbon pricing and pollution reduction in the United States. This is despite intransigence on the part of the federal government. But, because of the approach that has been adopted, it is possible for different states — and ultimately the federal government — to 'join' this process. In other circumstances, such as in attempting to ban child labour in cocoa production, governments have taken the lead with businesses joining later (Hawksley 2007).

The important point to recognise is that collaboration is not the norm. To achieve it you need to exhibit flexibility, to go to the negotiation table ready to concede some points, and agree to disagree on others. You don't need to have all your values in common, but on the specific partnership it is crucial that you agree on key points. There is a real need for *progressive* businesses and *pragmatic* governments (and NGOs) to forge partnerships based on shared value and common values.

Risk sharing

Entering any new partnership or business endeavour carries risks. But, when engaging with government, NGOs and local communities, these risks are higher because of the uncertainty involved. For many businesses, partnering with NGOs and communities is breaking new ground. The same is true with your partner organisations: they might be initially hesitant and cautious about 'getting into bed' with big business. This is why it is crucial that the partnership has a solid foundation in shared value creation and common values, built on personal relationships and trust. But, as with any partnership, these risks need to be acknowledged and they need to be shared.

A collaboration where one party provides all the funding and resources, while the other party assumes all of the risk, is not sustainable. If businesses are seen as a 'cash cow', then other partners are missing out on the more substantive contributions of skills and expertise, and corporate partners will not realise much gain. What is needed instead is a clear mechanism by which risks, as well as potential rewards or 'value creation', are shared between the parties. For NGOs it is much easier to be seen attacking corporate policies; this makes good headlines and helps fundraising. But, if NGOs are responsible and are genuinely committed to making a difference, then constructive engagement is essential. Equally companies can no longer simply dismiss complaints against them — they too need to become increasingly transparent and accountable to stakeholders and society This is why collaboration between companies, NGOs and governments can create shared value for all participants.

But this sort of partnership carries reputational and other risks for NGO partners, which your business needs to recognise and try to reduce. Equally, allowing an external group such as an NGO to come into your business, to understand how your internal processes work and to have access to commercially sensitive information, also carries a risk. These sorts of reputational risk are difficult to manage, which again emphasises the importance of personal and professional trust. There also needs to be clarity about the limits of engagement and on how disputes will be resolved.

For other risks, such as the financial risks if the project fails, or for liabilities resulting from partnership activities, it is crucial that these risks are shared equitably. Often in partnerships there is no connection between risks and rewards, which makes it difficult to make 'investment' decisions. Not every initiative will work out. Some partnerships might fail for purely external reasons and it is crucial to work out in advance how these problems will be dealt with. At a wider level, both sides need to recognise that the other side is also taking risks; in negotiations you should be proactive in identifying, discussing and strategising to reduce these risks from the outset. Once these risks are managed, project partners are much more able to invest in innovation and in developing new projects, on the solid foundation of shared value creation and common values.

Implementing collaboration

Implementing collaboration relies on good planning. Effective partnerships are built on a common definition of the problems to be addressed and a shared effort to resolve these problems. Partners need to contribute the key skills and expertise that they have. There is little point in companies trying to conduct activities outside of their mandate and core competences. Equally, NGOs and governments need to recognise the extent and limits of their own capabilities. It is in the crossover of skills and the sharing of expertise that good partnerships are founded.

But there is more to implementing an effective collaboration than a matching of needs and expertise. Risks must be identified and shared – and the value created needs to be likewise identified and shared. The old model, of companies contributing cash but not competences, fails to deliver value for either partner. Instead, companies, NGOs, government and local communities need to work together – coalescing around a set of common values – to solve problems too complex to be solved alone. If these partnerships are to be sustainable, shared value needs to be created. Each partner needs to gain something: profit, enhanced community life, environmental protection, a healthier society or improved legitimacy.

Putting a partnership into place, and managing it in practice, is a real challenge. In all likelihood your company will have to play a leading role in managing the relationship – indeed this is advisable to ensure that you gain the maximum benefit. Here you will need to 'find the right balance between mutual commitment and compatibility' with each partner, gaining from each 'complementarily of expertise that the different sectors can bring' (Findlay 2007). This will mean managing different power relationships that arise throughout the process, as different partners seek control of their own area of responsibility. Conflicts can arise because of misunderstandings over whose responsibilities lie where – reinforcing the need for good planning.

Equally, issues of *accountability* and *decision-making* should be well established and agreed on in advance. A common complaint from businesses partnering with UN agencies is that there is no accountability within UN agencies, as decisions are made by committee, which tends to be a slow process. If you are managing, or even participating, in a partnership with a UN agency or NGO, then you need to acknowledge that they will have different decision-making processes. Similarly, companies often complain that the accounting standards of NGO partners are insufficient for company purposes, which is a risk as well as an opportunity for capacity sharing as part of a partnership. The accountability and decisive capacity of companies is perhaps one of the most useful contributions that companies can make to partnerships. NGOs and other partners stand to benefit significantly from the contribution of these skills to their operations.

Making all this happen in reality is not easy. But, by having a clear plan and division of responsibilities (as well as risks) set out in advance, the chances of success can be improved. As with implementing the rest of the CSR agenda, companies need to use their core competences, in this case their ability to operate efficiently and accountably, and contribute these to the collaboration. Sometimes these partnerships will involve close collaboration; sometimes distance is required to ensure legitimacy and effectiveness. One example of how this has worked, delivering value to shareholders, society and the environment, is the partnership between Montana Exploradora and AMAC.

Case study: AMAC and Montana Exploradora — community consultation for environmental protection

The Marlin gold mine, operated by Montana in western Guatemala,[32] has experienced some problems and obstructions in dealing with the local community. Many of these problems relate to community concerns about the impact of the mine on local water supplies. This tension between the mine and community groups was causing operational problems and threatened Montana's licence to operate. Without continued community consent, the mine would have had practical difficulties in mining gold and in gaining government permits, especially on environmental criteria. Equally, the uncertainty about the quality of local water supplies was a cause of considerable distress to the community and it was in everybody's interests to resolve this dispute amicably.

Montana, as part of its environmental impact assessment (necessary to conduct mining operations in Guatemala), undertook to establish a community monitoring programme. The idea was that community engagement would help to reduce fears and lead to better communication between stakeholders. To achieve this Montana initially tried to establish an 'in-house' system for monitoring local water quality, using its core competences in environmental management to take samples and test water quality. However, this approach failed because it lacked legitimacy in the eyes of the local community, who remained distrustful of test results from the company. The company was then proactive in seeking solutions to this problem, as James Schenck, Manager for Sustainable Development explained: 'we took time to talk with people, we listened and people explained why it was not working, for diverse reasons . . . then we sat together and started looking at solutions'.

While looking for solutions, Montana maintained that the mine was not polluting local water supplies, yet the community continued to complain of water pollution. It is important to realise here that, for the local community, perception is reality and that the lack of trust in the company was undermining its efforts. As Bernarda Elizalde notes:

> Sometimes there are issues with water quality, and it is then important that these are solved quickly, for everyone's interests. Sometimes the perception and reality are not the same — so it is important to have someone there to test and be trusted.[33]

This realisation led Montana to support the establishment of an independent community-based environmental monitoring committee (AMAC).[34] In essence this is a communication bridge between the company and the communities and, because of the lack of trust, it is necessarily a distant partnership in some respects. But what we see is that, through AMAC, the communities have been empowered to work in a strongly independent manner with Montana Exploradora to share common values, creating an outcome that is good for the community and the environment. This model, of partnership on common environmental goals, also serves as a model for constructive dialogue between communities and the extractive industries.

Montana contributes finance through an indirect funding mechanism that guarantees the independence of AMAC. Equally, the company has contributed training and capacity building for AMAC, sending its environmental experts to AMAC to assist them in developing their skills and competences.

The crucial aspect is that there are values in common between Montana and AMAC: a commitment to environmental protection and to promoting dialogue between the company and local communities. Achieving these goals would have been impossible alone, so a collaboration to create shared value was the right solution.

How AMAC works

AMAC is a proudly independent community-based environmental monitoring committee, which brings together nine communities in the municipalities of San Miguel Ixtahuacan and Sipacapa, western Guatemala. Established in 2005, after a wide consultation process, the local communities stipulated that they would engage with AMAC if (IFC 2007):

- AMAC focuses on communities directly impacted by the mine's operation

- Other groups could participate to provide technical or other support to AMAC, but the control of the environmental monitoring remains in the hands of the local communities

- The initiative is independent from the company and the work of AMAC is not paid for directly by the company

- The company listens and responds to AMAC's suggestions

Thus AMAC is based on nine representatives of the municipalities, as well as one individual nominated by the Catholic Church in San Miguel (until the end of 2007, at which stage the church withdrew from AMAC). To support this group, external experts are used as resource people, currently including an environmental scientist, a private consultant and technical support from the Universidad San Carlos (in Guatemala City). Notably, a neutral third party, an NGO from the Universidad San Carlos, was considered to be the institutional conduit for the funds, given by Montana and the International Finance Corporation (IFC), to finance the programme activities of AMAC including the external advisers as well as the laboratory costs for water sampling. The Foundation has absolutely no role in the monitoring function; its role is to avoid a direct link between AMAC and Montana from a financial perspective. Montana has no jurisdiction over AMAC's decisions. This distance is important in helping to establish the independence of AMAC – thus giving it local legitimacy and trust – which was the key aspect missing from the company-led effort.

On a practical level AMAC and Montana conduct joint water sampling in the areas surrounding the mine. These results are then sent to separate laboratories for analysis and the results are discussed and compared directly with the results reported by Montana, the baseline data collected by the company, and national and international standards. Again, this is evidence of an 'independent partnership'. The two parties cooperate where it is useful, but retain independence to ensure that the findings are credible. In practice the company and the community are building trust and understanding through this partnership, from which both Montana and local communities benefit. In a sense AMAC is a conduit or meeting place where Montana and local communities can discuss their concerns, focused initially on environmental protection, but with the benefits spreading much wider.

The impact of this partnership on community relations has been profound; in the words of one community member: 'Before we used to block the road and come up with sticks and rocks — now we have opened a dialogue and can talk'.[35]

Shared benefits of collaboration

The result of having AMAC in place is that when members of the local community identify what they perceive to be a problem, they contact AMAC directly. AMAC then takes samples of the water in collaboration with Montana, thus engaging the company in a constructive way. This benefits the community, as they now have a channel through which to voice concerns and to gain credible information on water quality. The company also benefits by securing its licence to operate and reducing the risk of forced closures due to community distrust. Though a strongly 'independent partnership', this is a partnership that creates shared value for the community and the company. It is also a partnership that relies heavily on investing in building trust between the partners.

Value for the community

What AMAC means in practical terms for the local community is that concerns can be resolved quickly and without conflict. For example, a recent event led to perceived contamination of a waterway. Local residents, understandably concerned at this, contacted AMAC which took water samples. AMAC was able to quickly report that the contamination was only visual and that the water was still safe for agricultural purposes, enabling the community to continue their agricultural activities. AMAC then discussed the event with Montana, which had also taken samples, and an action plan was agreed to resolve the contamination within 24 hours.

Examples such as this have a very direct impact on the community. Also useful are the indirect benefits of having a community organisation that can respond to community needs. For instance AMAC sampled water, believed by residents to be contaminated and causing hair loss among children. Formerly this health scare would have been blamed on the company and would have led to animosity but not to a solution. However, AMAC was able to report, and be trusted when it did report, that the hair loss was caused by poor hygiene. Because of the community-based nature of AMAC the organisation was then able to mobilise NGO contacts to provide sanitation and health training, benefiting the community and saving an unnecessary confrontation with the company.

Value for the company

Montana also benefits from having AMAC as an independent but trusted partner. Increasingly, mining operations rely on local consent and a 'social' licence to operate that goes beyond traditional permitting. With the continued concerns about water quality and the mine's impact on the environment, the legal licence to operate for Montana was insecure. Moreover, community distrust and discontent — the 'block the road and come up with sticks and rocks' approach — was a real threat to company staff and operations.

One example given by James Schenck from Montana is of AMAC members witnessing a drilling rig spilling some oil on the ground, which was seen during a routine water sampling visit. 'My environmental manager was angry, the AMAC members were angry . . . they wanted a solution and to write a letter of complaint.' Having the open dialogue enabled the company to resolve the spillage within 24 hours 'so when they came back two days later it was a case of writing a letter noting that the problem had been solved'.[36]

For Montana, having AMAC as a partner gives it a channel for dialogue and discussion. With a partner that has local legitimacy, maintained through its strongly independent stance, Montana is able to settle disputes and disagreements amicably. In many cases these concerns do not relate to water contamination directly: for example, when the company built an airstrip nearby. But having an established partner in place enabled consultation rather than conflict.

This 'social' licence to operate is increasingly important in the mining industry, and the AMAC partnership is in essence a formal channel for a wider corporate approach of 'how you choose to work with people, of favouring process and transparency, rather than threats' (James Schenck). This is an approach that needs to rest on common values between partners and can create value for companies and communities.

Common values but strong independence

What we see in this example of partnership is that partners do not need to agree on everything. In fact, part of the success of AMAC is its independence from Montana — this makes it a trusted player in the community and helps it retain legitimacy. But the partnership works because there is a common value where it matters — a focus on preventing water pollution. Because of this common goal, the two partners are able to cooperate in a way that creates value for the company and for the community.

This partnership is more innovative than the traditional business approach of donating to an NGO. Any international NGO would probably have had the same problems of legitimacy as Montana did, especially if it was perceived to be paid by Montana. Likewise, attempting to solve the problem using core competences alone proved impossible. But, by contributing the company's core competence in environmental testing to AMAC, as an independent community group, Montana has been able to secure its licence to operate and alleviate many community concerns about water quality. Most encouragingly, this partnership is now growing to cover new areas of community consultation and engagement, further benefiting the company through securing its operations and creating value for the community.

Conclusions

Collaboration can form creative solutions to persistent problems. There are always problems and areas where companies are not expert, problems that businesses cannot solve alone. This is especially likely in the 'hard' industries where company operations often impact on communities and environments that are remote, difficult and very different from the home environment of the company. The right solution is then to find opportunities to create shared value with partners, remembering that these partnerships need to be founded on some common values. Partners need to have a shared understanding of the problem and come up with a common definition of how this can be resolved together.

This is why strategic relationships are needed. These are partnerships that are focused on the specific needs and problems at hand, defining a solution to these problems that mobilises the skills and competences of each partner. The old solution, of charitable donations, does not directly address the needs and issues of the 'hard' industries working today in the developing world and difficult environments. Innovative, strategic partnerships are needed to mobilise the skills of partners to solve difficult problems.

In implementing these collaborations, risk sharing is crucial. Each partner — an NGO, a government agency, a community as well as the company — needs to have a stake in the outcome. These risks will not always be equal, but they need to be shared. It is only where collaborations are based on common values, shared risks and shared benefits that they can be effectively implemented.

Partnerships are not easy — they are difficult and require management and commitment. But for solving problems that cannot be solved individually, for mobilising various competences and resources to create shared value, relationships offer real opportunities for implementing CSR in the 'hard' industries.

4

Operate globally–impact locally

The products and services that are sold in the rich world do not automatically have a market in the poor world. But any company that ignores 80% of the global population does so at its peril. This market has been termed the 'bottom of the pyramid' by C.K. Prahalad (2004). But to meet this market, to deliver goods and services that are affordable to people who are currently under-served, requires translating operations from the global to the local. This means embedding your supply chain, market research, sales and service in the local community. Doing this effectively requires companies to learn the lessons of the last two chapters, leveraging their core competences and collaborating based on common values. But it also requires corporations to transform their global operations into local operations – not just their manufacturing but also their management, career opportunities, market research and customer focus – in order to produce goods and services that serve both rich and poor markets. This approach, of creating value in previously untapped markets, holds considerable growth potential – well beyond the potential growth of 'mature' markets (Weiser *et al.* 2006).

By taking your global business to the local level, you place your company in a position to take advantage of new trends, of emerging growth opportunities and to gain access to literally billions of under-served customers and suppliers. Consumers also benefit, by gaining access to a wider range of lower-cost and higher-quality goods and services, as well as enhanced employment opportunities. This sort of creation of public good through the pursuit of private profit is exactly what Adam Smith was talking about when he discussed how economic growth created public good.

But the benefits of 'going local' extend well beyond the traditional economic measures and go beyond simple outsourcing and offshoring. Going local also develops markets and builds communities, engaging those who have missed out from the benefits of globalisation. Paul Collier (2007) in his arresting book *The Bottom Billion* discusses how the traditional barriers to development — the resource curse, illiberal politics and corruption — can be overcome through active engagement with business. For today's companies there is a real potential to help this 'bottom billion', as well as the bottom line. But this is not easy and it does require a change in how companies do business in the developing world. By working in partnership with local suppliers and providing opportunities for local employees, managers and consumers, companies can empower communities and drive development.

The opportunities that exist for new goods and services in under-served markets are immense. Moreover, when companies engage poor communities as partners, they are making an investment in creating future markets. This is the sort of win–win example of CSR that places the responsibilities to shareholders, in both present and future returns, at the centre, while also contributing to wider social development. In fact I would argue that any company that continues to focus on just its home market is failing to take its long-term responsibility to shareholders into account. In an increasingly global economy the 'licence to operate' will come under threat for companies that only 'offshore' without also expanding the opportunities for local staff, suppliers and managers to engage with what a corporation has to offer. In the long run, not going local excludes companies from the large growth markets of the developing world, which is surely not in the interests of shareholders or society.

Localising operations is not easy; it requires companies to be very clear in what their core competences are; it requires clear collaboration to develop and build new competences; but, most important, going local is a complete approach. It is irresponsible for companies, both to their shareholders and to society, to try to sell goods and services to the 'bottom of the pyramid' without also engaging with those consumers and suppliers. While many books tell us there is a 'fortune' to be made by doing this, what is often forgotten is the difficult — yet vital — process of empowering these consumers. This is why, to borrow from Joseph Stiglitz (2007), *Making Globalisation Work* is important for rich as well as poor. But, in order to create genuine economic opportunities for the company and for consumers, businesses need to 'go local': to understand the market they are working in, to engage constructively and to take their responsibilities seriously at all levels. This is a hard task, but it is one that can create enormous corporate opportunities.

Beyond offshoring

'Offshoring' has become a contentious topic, seen in parts of the rich world as destroying jobs and increasing 'corporate greed', seen in parts of the poor world as exploitation and a return to colonialism. There are undoubtedly negative impacts from offshoring (or *délocalisation* as it is inelegantly labelled in French). But the fact is that moving jobs, services and manufacturing to low-cost centres (globalising) can have positive impacts – in both the rich and the poor worlds. Where companies have perhaps been unfortunate is in failing to adequately communicate the benefits of offshoring and outsourcing in terms of cheaper and better products, more reliable supply chains and improved economic development in the developing world. This is a case of communicating how it is that globalisation does work as much as it is a case of changing how globalisation works (Wolf 2005). But for the benefits of globalisation to endure, to prevent a 'race to the bottom' towards the lowest-cost centres with the fewest labour laws and environmental regulations, companies need to look *beyond offshoring*.

The gains to business from offshoring and outsourcing have largely been accrued already. As one-off cost cuts and efficiency gains, companies have seen benefits, although these have not always been as great as they promised to be, since costs in popular offshoring centres such as India and China have risen rapidly. To sustain cost reductions and to ensure that you benefit from a presence in the developing world, it is important to look at:

- What opportunities exist to develop new markets and how this will impact on your existing responsibilities to staff, suppliers, customers and the environment

- What you hope to achieve by offshoring and outsourcing – is it just cost reduction or are there strategic interests as well?

- Which corporate values, beliefs and goals fit well with the local culture; what are you prepared to compromise on and what are you not?

It is crucial that your company approaches these issues strategically – in light of the social and environmental obligations (and opportunities) that you have identified as important to your company (Pyndt and Pedersen 2005). How you go about offshoring *the process* is crucial. If jobs are to be lost, you need to be open with your staff and suppliers about how it will affect them, what sort of support will be provided and give them the information they need to make decisions about their future. Irresponsible corporate behaviour, using the threat of job cuts to extract state subsidies, often does greater harm to the company than the short-term gain. Consumers and the media are very quick to point out any inconsistencies in company statements from strategy. For example Google – a company that explicitly states its goal to 'do no evil' — was roundly criticised for allowing limited state censorship in its Chinese subsidiary search engine. The fact that Google was allowing 'less' censorship than other companies was not discussed in the media, only its failure to live up to its stated commitments.

This is where the responsible corporation takes a long-term, strategic view of offshoring. Often non-price benefits can be gained by 'near-shoring' or other alternative strategies. These mix the benefits of proximity to market with the cost savings of offshoring; unlikely offshoring hubs such as Malta are gaining popularity (Dempsey 2007). In terms of serving the 'bottom of the pyramid' companies need to look at poor consumers not as cheap, easily replaced labour, but as partners in the firms' success (as with all other staff) and in the long term as potential consumers. Much offshoring to date has failed to create enduring economic opportunities for local staff, but exceptional companies such as Gildan (discussed in the case study below) show that there is a clear business case for creating local opportunities. Many of the allegations levelled against companies, as being exploitative and endangering worker rights, are easily confronted when you treat local workers with dignity and respect — as partners in growth and progress.

Offshoring and outsourcing responsibly is a potential source of strategic advantage for companies, building cumulative advantage over your competitors while investing in the long-term profitability of your company. By taking a strategic perspective, offshoring can become much more than a one-off cost-cutting measure. Instead it can drive business growth by embedding the business in new markets, exposing it to new opportunities and enabling the company to increase its returns to shareholders and society. To achieve this you need to focus on three key principles: create local opportunities, 'go local' and manage your local social contribution.

Creating local opportunities

In a competitive business environment, your staff and suppliers are your key constituents in the drive for good corporate citizenship. If you are to deliver strong returns to shareholders, you need to treat your staff as the most important business asset; likewise, your suppliers and wider society must be engaged as partners. The concept that you need to treat your staff well, as key business assets, is not new in management thinking. But it is notable that this idea of an inclusive corporation, which provides opportunities for upward movement for staff, has not been well adopted in the offshoring movement.

If we think of staff as constituents in a corporation, having different tiers of staffing is a form of second-class corporate citizenship. This disenfranchises workers; they no longer feel that they have a stake in, or responsibility to, the company. This is hardly the best way to make sure you get the most out of your most valuable asset. Likewise, suppliers are crucial business partners, how they work with your company – in collaboration – will have a big impact on the success of your business. A short-sighted view that emphasises only immediate profit will ultimately be unsustainable. Your dealings with society and other stakeholders must also be responsible, contributing to the economic (and social) development of the countries in which you work. This is why it is essential that responsible corporations create meaningful opportunities for staff and suppliers.

Staff opportunities

When you begin to look at staffing of multinationals working in the developing world, there is the usual structure of business and HR, between 'local' and 'expatriate' staff. Characteristically, expatriate staff are on large salaries with a lot of benefits, encouraged to work for a few years in a 'emerging' market as a way of gaining experience which they then bring back to 'head office'. Local staff are well paid by local standards, but few opportunities tend to exist to move out of their local office and into the mainstream of the organisation. There is a clear divide between the 'central' roles in head office and the 'peripheral' roles in local offices. This divide is even greater when you look at multinationals working through subsidiaries, joint ventures or local holding companies. While not an absolute rule, this is often how HR is seen to be managed in offshoring.

The impacts of this system are twofold. First, the head office is cut off from identifying the emerging trends and opportunities in the developing world, as there are no 'upward' mechanisms for knowledge, ideas and innovation to flow. While expatriate staff do gain an understanding during their time in the 'local' office, this can never make up for local knowledge. Second, companies fail to gain the loyalty and trust of their local staff; the most talented locals see the glass ceiling and steer well away. This is even true in low-skill manufacturing and process jobs, where recruitment continues to be a problem because people recognise that there is a lack of upward opportunities.[37]

The responsible corporation recognises its obligation to provide equal opportunities not only at head office, but also within its global operations. The strategic corporation also recognises the opportunities inherent in providing career opportunities for good staff. Fifty years ago gender pay disparity was accepted and commonplace, but no company would accept such inequalities in its head office now. So too should the forward-looking company try to find ways to attract the best talent, wherever in the world they might work, providing the opportu-

Box 3 **A living wage? Novartis and a novel approach to pay**

Novartis, a Swiss-based pharmaceutical company, has operations in many areas of the developing world, where the market rate of pay is not always enough to meet the requirements of a family. Employing 100,000 people in 140 countries means operating in locations where labour and employment laws are insufficient. Thus there is a need to be proactive, to go beyond minimum requirements, in order to be seen as a responsible corporation.

Recognising the need to go beyond national laws on minimum wages as part of its commitment to the UN Global Compact, Novartis sought to implement a system of the 'living wage' throughout its operations. This living wage reflects the cost of a basket of goods that is considered to provide an adequate standard of living in each area in which the company operates. Calculating this basket of goods was not easy, especially as Novartis was the first company in the pharmaceutical industry to implement such a system. But, by putting in place a 'living wage' approach to pay, Novartis was able to demonstrate to local communities and host countries its commitment to conducting business responsibly. This in turn helped the company illustrate how it was putting the UN Global Compact into practice inside its operations.

The living wage initiative is part of a corporate approach to CSR that aims for Novartis: 'to be recognised as an innovative, ethical and trustworthy company, fostering a culture where employees are expected to behave ethically, not just lawfully'.

Such an approach is essential for proactive companies, looking to operate in the developing world, which recognise that their responsibilities extend beyond the national minimums. This helps to counter the arguments of a 'race to the bottom' normally made against localising operations. By localising operations responsibly, value is also created for the company, in terms of an enhanced 'licence to operate', as explained by Klaus Leisinger, President of the Novartis Foundation for Sustainable Development:

> The key benefit from the Novartis Company is derived by patients from the value of the medicine. If the corporate deliverables in the context of the key competence are created with integrity (e.g. living the spirit of the Global Compact) then this is guaranteeing the licence to operate.[38]

This licence to operate positions responsible companies to take advantage of the opportunities of localising operations, without being seen to be 'taking advantage' of workers and local partners.

nities and support for staff to develop and contribute to long-term company profit. This also enhances the company's 'licence to operate', especially in the developing world, because it is seen to be investing in economic and social development. These investments in human resources are responsible decisions, based on the goal of delivering long-term financial returns to shareholders, while also benefiting staff as key stakeholders.

Who dares, twins: suppliers and CSR

In the outsourcing debate many companies have pursued short-term contracts, offering the lowest price with few questions asked. From a purely financial perspective, many of these deals have gone wrong, as over-stretched suppliers have been unable to meet ever higher demands for ever decreasing prices. 'Just in time' supply chains have become just too late. From a social and environmental perspective, these sorts of supplier arrangement have encouraged the 'race to the bottom' for the lowest levels of worker rights and environmental protection. It is not necessary to recount here the major brands, especially in the textile industry, that have suffered great business damage in the pursuit of marginally lower production costs. Equally, some companies' efforts to be seen as 'green' or 'fair-trade' brands have been damaged significantly by one rogue external supplier.[39] What is important to recognise is that long-term strategy needs to be applied in partnerships with suppliers (as well as customers), which is why responsible corporations look for the opportunities inherent in twinning with suppliers. This is built around building 'arcs of integration' between suppliers, the company and ultimately with consumers. There is 'consistent evidence' that closer connection between suppliers, companies and consumers leads to improved commercial and environmental performance (Frohlich and Westbrook 2001).

If we take some of the key lessons from outsourcing, from a purely financial perspective, the lessons learned are that companies should:

- Develop cost savings while avoiding isolated performance targets
- Work closely with customers to drive process improvements
- Use information technology to track products throughout the chain in real time

These same lessons from outsourcing can also be applied to how you work with suppliers to ensure that your social and environmental responsibilities are met. It is important to develop metrics, verifiable indicators, which track how your suppliers are meeting the social and environmental goals of your company. These metrics need to be monitored and evaluated just as thoroughly as quality and other metrics. We see this happening already in countries such as China, where — contrary to globalisation's sceptics — we see increasing environmental standards as a result of voluntary benchmarking by international firms (Christmann and Taylor 2001).

In taking your global supply chain to the local level you should be careful not to distance evolving customer needs from your supply chain. This is where IT can be used to track and control the source of products. Just as RFID (radio frequency identification) tags are used by businesses to track inventories, these same monitoring systems can be used to safeguard your supply chain. Internal and external auditors can help identify (and resolve) issues early on, before the supply chain and the business is exposed to risk. For instance, in the textile trade there are a number of organisations that help companies to assure they are adhering to labour and environmental standards. Implementing assurance programmes effectively takes the lessons from the last chapter on partnerships, applying them in a local context through the use of 'twinning', sharing responsibility and information with suppliers to deliver improved financial, and social, outcomes.

'Going local'

Missing from many attempts at CSR yet crucial to success is a focus on community development and genuine 'localisation'. This does not mean that companies need to act as aid agencies or charities, or that they give up their original identity and purpose. On the contrary: companies need to invest their expertise and capital in sustainable business development, both within the company and with suppliers and society. This *process* of 'going local' can begin by working with existing suppliers and by placing greater focus on catalysing local business development. These sorts of initiative have been very successful in the extractive industries in the Former Soviet Union, an area in which I have been closely involved as an adviser to Localis.[40] What we have learned is that the extractive industries have considerable expertise in operating in unclear or difficult legal and political structures and that they know how to make the best use of capital investments. These are skills that can be usefully applied in supporting local businesses.

Community development of this kind needs to be economically viable in the short term and in the long term must be able to operate without further assistance. It must be sustainable and profitable, both for the responsible corporation and for local business. Yet we also need to realise that often small levels of assistance, whether technical, financial, expertise or simply securing the 'first contract', are what is lacking for many businesses operating in the developing world. Creating a changed business climate in the developing world, and the future for

CSR is not in creating false economies. Rather it is about catalysing local economic development by encouraging businesses to do what they already do well, and applying it at a local level. The Anglo Zimele case in Chapter 2 demonstrates this well.

'Going local' recognises that, for companies working in the developing world, the focus of CSR policy needs to be on providing a strong return on investment – both in contributing to the bottom line by reducing costs as well as by developing the business profile. Yet this focus on short-term profitability is, by itself, insufficient. Businesses around the world are coming under increasing pressure to deal with the environmental and social impacts that their operations create. This is especially the case in the developing world, with growing inequality in both income and power. While rising income inequality is a natural, indeed necessary, corollary of the transition towards a market economy, more problematic has been the increase in power inequality.

While businesses do not deserve to be blamed for all the ills of the developing world, it is reasonable to expect their contribution to be positive. Companies working in poor regions of the world are now expected to find ways to ensure that their economic contribution is generally positive – both to the state and within the communities in which they operate. Governments as well as consumers have raised their expectations, and companies need to respond. This means that companies need to formulate a CSR policy that ensures they:

- Identify, through risk analysis, how issues such as the environment, social inequality and corruption impact on their operations, and then use CSR and localisation as tools to address these issues

- Publicise the positive impacts that their investment is having in the economic and social life of the regions in which they work, by showing the employment that is being created and the local economic opportunities for suppliers

- Constantly expand CSR policy and localise operations to increase the positive impacts that the company has on local and regional development

Successful examples of how going local can work include the community development initiatives of the BTC (Baku–Tbilisi–Ceyhan) pipeline, which focused on catalysing local development. The companies involved did this in a way that was relevant and appropriate to the local communities. By setting up local businesses, communities begin to see the benefits of the business but, unlike charitable giving, these economic impacts have a strong multiplier effect, creating downstream jobs and driving genuine economic development (IFC 2006). Likewise, the local manufacture of safety gloves in Azerbaijan by women working from home has reduced company costs and created local employment. However, implementing these sorts of initiative – and ensuring that they are sustainable – is difficult.

We need to accept that the challenges in implementing localisation are considerable. Currently, much of the CSR that occurs is charity-based, responding to requests by local mayors and elites. This has meant that money has been spent, and continues to be spent, on projects of little mutual commercial/community benefit. Companies are contributing cash but not expertise, in a form of spending that buys neither regional development nor local legitimacy. What this points out is the fine line between meeting state interests (which remains crucial) and contributing to local needs. Inevitably there is a need for compromise; companies must strike a balance between meeting the needs and demands of all their stakeholders: investors, host governments, employees and local communities. The right way to do this is by creating local opportunities and economic development, in a way that reduces company costs (and risks) while creating genuine local opportunities.

Local social contribution

Your business, no matter what industry it is in or wherever it is located, is part of a community. Part of being a responsible member of a community, anywhere in the world, is ensuring that you follow the rules and contribute to the community. It is crucial that the 'creative destruction' (Schumpeter 1942) of capitalism is seen locally to be having a creative and positive impact on society and the economy. This is where more broad conceptions of CSR come into play, with companies' 'licence to operate' being determined by the communities in which they work. At a wider level companies need healthy and functional societies in which to operate and it is important to recognise the positive (and potentially negative) impacts that business has on society. This goes beyond following local laws; it is also about encouraging improved standards – against corruption, in favour of environmental protection or in ensuring employment opportunities. This is where companies operating in developing countries can make a positive contribution, by introducing higher environmental standards and improved business systems to ensure social compliance – beyond minimum legal standards.

Often companies are already making significant contributions to the communities and cultures in which they work. But we need to recognise that there are sometimes negative environmental and social 'externalities' associated with doing business. Good CSR policy and practice builds on these areas of weakness, identifying potential risks and problems and then resolving these issues in a strategic manner. The key is to balance the positive things that are already occurring with recognition – and then mitigation – of negative impacts. To put this into practice I have a three-step approach that I take with my clients in the extractive industries in the Former Soviet Union.

In looking to make a social contribution, the initial diagnostic is focused on working with company management and representatives of the community to:

- Identify local needs and issues through community consultation, then attempt to match these where possible with corporate objectives

- Review the company's existing community commitments and current policies

- Develop recommendations for future CSR initiatives that tie in with company strategy and community needs

This may sound slightly abstract, but when you go through the process you begin to realise, as does the community, that the company is already making a big contribution. Moreover, with a little adjustment of strategy, this contribution can be enhanced at little extra cost. In fact, I argue that CSR policies and social contributions have to be good investments. These are investments in a continued licence to operate, in reducing the risks of shutdowns and industrial disputes (very costly in any industry, especially so in the extractive industries) and in the future growth of the company. This is why social impacts and contributions need to be assessed against clear criteria, such as:

- The direct benefits to the local community, such as improving access to employment and educational opportunities

- Alignment of social well-being with corporate strategy, including reducing waste, improving productivity and ensuring staff security

- Creating 'shared value': for the company in terms of increased productivity, reduced costs or positive perceptions towards their project; for society in terms of increased employment opportunities, improved infrastructure and access

- Environmental impact: 'shared value' benefit focused on maintaining and where possible improving the health of the local environment

- Public relations: not just improving the perception of the company locally, but demonstrating to potential investors how the company is behaving responsibly

Achieving this social benefit needs to fit into the long-term, *strategic* CSR policy of your company. Supply chain management, localising operations, community consultation and social investments are all tools in implementing your strategic CSR policy. The scope for this sort of work is now expanding, as both communities and customers become more discerning in terms of which companies they choose to work with, buy from and supply. To keep ahead of these changing perceptions and new trends it is important to maintain regular consultation with NGOs and community groups, taking a participatory approach that can include staff surveys and consultation with government representatives.

For example, a mining company I work with in Kazakhstan has taken a proactive approach to CSR policy. Mine management consults regularly with the local community to ensure that company operations and policies reflect both corporate values and community concerns. Future business plans are discussed in light of community development strategies, in an attempt to create 'shared value' through shared infrastructure and education projects. Examples of how this strategy has been implemented include:

- Localising the supply chain, involving more local business in mine procurement, resulting in lower costs to the company and improved economic opportunities for the community

- Funding the provision of English language teachers at schools near the mine site

- Consultation on environmental initiatives: the planting of trees on site to reduce dust and noise pollution

Each of these solutions needs to be based on a solid, long-term business case for investment. But what we see from this and many other examples is that, once you begin to consider social responsibilities as part of business strategy, great opportunities exist for shared value creation. Making this work at a single mine site is one challenge, but meeting the multiple — at times conflicting — demands of different communities is a different challenge altogether. This is where the Gildan case study shows us how a multinational company, working in a competitive and often criticised industry, has been able to improve shareholder returns and increase the social good, through a dedicated strategy of operating globally and impacting locally..

Case study: Gildan

Gildan, a Montreal-based marketer and manufacturer of basic apparel (T-shirts, socks, fleeces, etc.), works in a cost-competitive, global industry with narrow margins. It is also an industry that is increasingly offshored and outsourced and one in which labour rights is a key concern. In 2004 Gildan was widely attacked by NGOs and in the media, because of problems associated with the closure of its *El Progreso* manufacturing plant in Honduras. The negative publicity surrounding the incident threatened company value; it put Gildan's 'licence to operate' in doubt and damaged the brand at a time when the company was looking to move into a strong retail focus for its products. The new management team decided that 'a key priority would be to repair our relationships with NGOs and local communities'.[41] This engagement with NGOs was part of an overall plan to rebuild trust and credibility in the company, placing CSR at the centre of corporate strategy. This included improving the corporate governance structure of the company and using CSR to build sustained competitive advantage.

From 2004 until today (2008), Gildan has gone from being a textile company which was campaigned against and targeted, to being a leading company demonstrating best practice in the industry. At the same time, its share value has increased fourfold, the company has delivered 30% annual earnings growth and it has expanded its operations, especially its manufacturing 'hubs' in Central America and the Caribbean. Making this strategy work has relied on Gildan's ability to localise its operations in new regions, while ensuring that corporate values are maintained and worker rights respected; all this while the company has grown from manufacturing 293 million garments a year in 2004, to close to 500 million in 2007. Key to Gildan's growth has been its investment in its human resources — creating local opportunities for team members and investing in their education, training and development.

CSR as corporate strategy

> We need to have a major advantage over our competitors; ours is providing the best value for the money . . . key to this is our human resources, having well-trained and motivated staff — social responsibility is a major aspect of that strategy (Cam Gentile, Executive Vice-President, Organisational Development & Change Management).[42]

Gildan operates in a price-competitive industry, with increasing competition from low-margin producers in Asia. To stay ahead of the competition, which can replicate simple product lines and buy in state-of-the-art equipment, Gildan has identified human resources as crucial to its continued growth and profitability. In localising manufacturing in Central America and the Caribbean, Gildan has invested heavily in local HR development, training and education. Because there is limited manufacturing capacity in much of this region, it has been necessary for Gildan not only to establish its factories, but also to invest in training skilled operators. This is part of a broad effort on the part of the company to encourage education for company employees as well as to support school lunch efforts by the World Food Programme, as part of a wider social contribution.

Initiatives such as its *Educatodos* (Education for All) programme, implemented in partnership with the Honduran Ministry of Education and USAID (US Agency for International Development), offer staff at manufacturing hubs the opportunity to complete their basic schooling. The opportunities this creates should not be underestimated; local staff I interviewed talked about how the *Educatodos* programme and in-house technical training allowed them to finish their schooling while working, and how this opened up new opportunities for promotion with Gildan. For instance, Adan Portillo, who had finished middle school, was able to gain further schooling and technical training on the job. Adan is now a production supervisor, a promotion that 'means a lot to me personally and for my family'. It has to be recognised that, given the skills shortage in Honduras, skilled and committed staff such as Adan are also key to Gildan's future growth.

Gildan has also invested in developing local technical training facilities that provide training for machinery operators, teaching useful skills such as welding, maintenance and repair. These skills were initially lacking in Honduras, so Gildan took the initiative of becoming the founding donor for the IPC (Central American Polytechnic Institute).[43] Recognising that education and training are key to successful investments in the developing world, CEO Glenn Chamandy was an active proponent of the IPC. As part of this ongoing commitment Gildan donates an annual scholarship fund to the IPC in Honduras. This provides the opportunity for 50 students from Central America to enrol in one-year programmes – clothing manufacturing, electricity or mechanics – while supporting the development of the IPC to provide technical training in the region. This involves a large financial commitment from Gildan, but it is seen as an investment in developing local capacity, which is central to the company's long-term growth plans:

> Some companies look at CSR as costing money; they shy away from it. We don't see CSR like that. CSR doesn't increase cost, it reduces cost . . . if you want to have maximum efficiency you need to have well-trained, committed, focused employees . . . all this spending converts into dollars and cents (Cam Gentile, Executive Vice-President, Organisational Development & Change Management).[44]

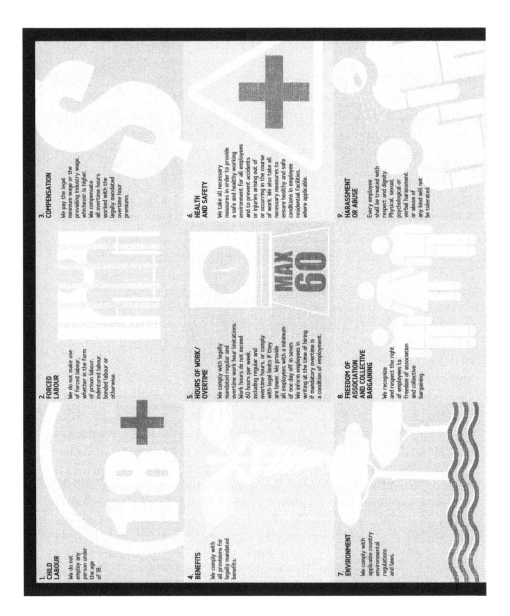

Figure 7 **Gildan's code of conduct**

Source: Copyright Gildan Activewear Inc.

Code of conduct

Wherever GILDAN operates, we are guided by this CODE of CONDUCT. All Gildan employees and business partners should adhere to these principles. These are set out above.

10. DISCIPLINE AND TERMINATION

Discipline and termination procedures are standardized and include a series of warnings prior to suspension or dismissal. Disciplinary procedures do not include the use of punitive deductions or forced resignations.

11. FREEDOM OF MOVEMENT

When authorized and under special circumstances (in an emergency or in a matter of personal urgency, death or illness of a family member), employees can leave the facility and are not penalized. Employees have free and reasonable access to drinking water and toilet facilities.

12. GRIEVANCE PROCEDURES

Employees are permitted to lodge grievances that are addressed in a systematic manner so as to protect employees' privacy and protect them from reprisals.

13. PREGNANCY

Female employees are not asked about their pregnancy status nor are they required to be tested for pregnancy. We abide by all local and international laws regarding working conditions for pregnant workers, including but not limited to rest breaks and adequate seating.

14. DISCRIMINATION

We do not discriminate in hiring, wages, benefits, advancement, discipline or termination on the basis of gender, race, religion, age, disability, physical appearance, pregnancy, sexual orientation, nationality, union affiliation, political opinion or social or ethnic origin.

15. DOCUMENTATION AND INSPECTION

We maintain on file such documentation as may be needed to demonstrate compliance with this CODE of CONDUCT, and shall make these documents available for GILDAN or its designated auditors for inspection.

GILDAN

Genuine opportunities exist for local staff to develop and grow their careers within the company. Young engineers are hired as first-line managers, given training in management skills and in company values then encouraged to grow within the company. For instance, the entire management of the Honduras hub comprises young Hondurans who are on the same salary scale as corporate managers in North America and participate in the same share-ownership plan. Providing these opportunities helps to minimise costly staff turnover, it enhances the company's 'licence to operate' and it helps reduce overall company costs by limiting the use of expensive expatriate staff. The opportunities for good local staff are immense, because of the fast growth of the company and because of the corporate commitment to social responsibility; it is possible for local staff to move upwards within the company; current directors and head office managers come from the offshore manufacturing hubs. This is very different from the 'outsourcing' model followed by many other textile companies, with a disconnect between local and foreign staff opportunities. It is good business practice, which is also socially responsible.

This same commitment to social responsibility, coupled with improving corporate performance, has been applied in the environmental arena. Because of the use of salt as a fixing agent in the dying process, textile plants have high water use and high levels of salt discharge. Gildan identified this as an environmental problem, even though it was compliant with existing environmental standards, and invested in developing a brine recovery system – all part of trying to 'go beyond minimum regulations – of wanting to be better than our competitors'.[45] By re-using the salt solution, Gildan is able to reduce the pollution emitted from the plant, while also saving business costs by staying ahead of environmental regulations and reducing overall salt use. The development of the 'Biotope' in Honduras has meant moving to biodegradable dyes and an investment in treatment ponds, but this investment is paying returns in reducing operating costs and positioning Gildan as a leader in environmental protection, which is increasingly important in the consumer market.

These social and environmental goals of creating local opportunities and contributing to local development are also integrated into supplier agreements with outside contractors. Gildan builds long-term relationships with suppliers and contractors: 'we don't have one-off contracts; the contractors we have are long-term relationships'.[46] Although Gildan is vertically integrated in its textile operations, it makes some use of outside sewing contractors. Ensuring that different suppliers and contractors meet their social responsibilities is increasingly important in the textile trade. Rather than take a pro forma approach, Gildan works closely with suppliers, supporting them and building shared value on the basis of common values. All these agreements are governed by Gildan's code of conduct, shown Figure 7.

This code of conduct aims to make Gildan 'best in class' for worker rights. There is a recognition that 'customers are becoming more demanding, not only in retail but also in business-to-business . . . volunteer initiatives quickly become law and that is when it is good to be at the head of the pack'.[47]

Gildan, having been on the wrong side of NGO activism in the past, is proactive in engaging NGOs. Gildan's social compliance programme has recently gained accreditation with the Fair Labor Association (FLA), recognising the company's success in adhering to the code of conduct and progressive labour practices and making it the first Canadian company and Canadian manufacturer to receive such recognition. Management systems, such as an anonymous complaints procedure, environmental monitoring and training modules, are all entered into a CSR database. This allows managers to monitor and evaluate performance against the code of conduct. Crucial to implementing this at a local level is engagement with NGOs and local communities.

NGO and community engagement

As part of the response to the negative publicity surrounding the *El Progreso* plant closure, Gildan entered into a dialogue with the Canadian-based Maquila Solidarity Network (MSN) and other NGOs, in an effort to resolve concerns about worker rights and plant closure practices. Laurence Sellyn, Chief Financial and Administrative Officer, travelled to Toronto to meet with the MSN leadership in an attempt to understand their concerns and to build dialogue:

> I went there with some trepidation — but we built trust: we found that we had similar values at the core, we had similar aims and we had trust . . . But I also knew that we would only win her [MSN's president's] trust through our actions.[48]

Gildan and MSN entered into a partnership, working together to create an action plan for remediation for submission to the FLA. This detailed how redundant workers would receive preferential reintegration into other sewing plants in Honduras and entailed Gildan committing to good practice in future closures. Building this relationship with MSN required commitment from very senior levels within the company, but ultimately the relationship relied on substance. Having built levels of trust, MSN found that it was able to achieve its goals without resorting to publicity: 'As other situations have come up, MSN now has a pipeline to communicate with us; they do not need to publicise — they just need to pick up the phone'.[49]

For instance, a more recent complaint, regarding an outside contractor, was raised directly with Gildan by some NGOs. This complaint was about the contractor not complying with the code of conduct. From the outset there was a complete commitment by the leadership of the company to resolve this problem – it bought in external auditors to address the issue – resulting in a resolution of the problem quickly and effectively. As far as MSN and other NGOs are concerned, there is no sort of campaigning that could have achieved this aim so effectively. For Gildan, the open pathway of communication allows the company to become aware of issues quickly, for these concerns to then be resolved, further strengthening the relationship between Gildan and the NGO community.

On a non-operational level, Gildan contributes 1% of pre-tax profits earned in Canada to the charitable sector. This giving is focused on humanitarian issues, as well as youth and education, focused on the communities in which the company operates. For example, a long-term partnership with *Dans la rue* (On the Street), which focuses on Montreal's homeless youth, involves staff volunteer time as well as financial contributions. While there is no clear link here between company operations and the giving, Gildan considers it an important part of its long-term commitment to Montreal, as with all communities in which the company operates, enhancing its 'licence to operate' and helping to attract and retain good staff.

This same commitment is also present at the Central American and Caribbean hubs. Gildan is open to proposals from local communities and staff about how it can improve its social contribution. A recent example is of a school, close to the Rio Nance production facility in Honduras, which lacked adequate classrooms. Based on the concept of a shared commitment the local community donated the land for the new school. Working in partnership with a local NGO, Gildan then contributed the financing for a new five-room school building – as part of a wider government and World Bank effort to improve basic education in Honduras. However, this is not just a one-off donation; it is seen as an investment in improving local community relations and governmental engagement. By taking the lead on issues such as education, core to the future development of both Gildan and the countries in which it works, Gildan helps to build long-term relationships and trust in host countries. The presence of high-level staff from the Ministry of Education at the inauguration of the school is testament to the impact that locally appropriate, co-financed projects such as the Rio Nance School can have on community and government relations. It also helps in providing education and training for future staff and supervisors – staff who are essential as Gildan continues to expand its operations and looks to employ, literally, thousands more staff in the coming years.

Local operations: local opportunities

> I was 39 years old, with three children – in this society that makes it very difficult to get a job. I attended the IPC on a Gildan scholar-

> ship — completing a Diploma in Production. I then did an intern-
> ship with Gildan, and they offered me a job; I was very surprised
> and very glad . . . I enjoy my work; Gildan is a very respectful com-
> pany and I am proud to work here (Guadalupe Banegas, Produc-
> tion Supervisor, San Jose Sewing facility, Honduras).[50]

There is a common misconception that work in the textile trade is unskilled. In
fact, textile operators require a lot of training, and the need for mechanics and
other trained staff, as well as shift and production supervisors, makes human
resources crucial. Besides being important for the company, localising operations and providing training opens up great opportunities for local staff. On my
visits to site operations I was constantly impressed by how much local staff aspire
to, and achieve, promotion within Gildan. Not only are production jobs given to
local staff, but also core management, communications and human resources
roles are filled by talented Central American and Caribbean citizens. For example, all the locally based directors and the regional vice-president are from Central America and the Caribbean. Sometimes promotion to these roles requires
upskilling and further education, which is where the education and training
offered internally (and externally through the IPC and with NGO partners)
demonstrates the investment in human resources that is necessary in localising
operations in a responsible manner. Besides being more cost effective than expatriate workers, locally engaged staff have a greater appreciation of the culture in
which they work.

In implementing a CSR agenda, understanding the local culture is crucial. For
instance, implementing the code of conduct for all workers in Gildan required
working across four languages and many borders.

> Finding the right way to communicate the message, of the Code of
> Conduct, was a challenge. These are sophisticated concepts and
> applying them can be difficult — for example, harassment is a cul-
> tural issue; we have zero tolerance, so we need to change behaviour
> (Claudia Sandoval, Regional Communications Director).[51]

Changing cultural norms and introducing new ways of working is never easy, but
it is especially challenging for outsiders. This is where someone who comes from
the culture, who has lived and worked in it all his or her life, is much better
equipped to implement company policy. Recognising this, Gildan has placed
almost all managerial roles at its 'hubs' in the hands of local individuals, many of
whom have been promoted within the company and all of whom participate in
the same salary and share-ownership scheme as Montreal-based employees.

Because of a commitment to complete offshoring not only of manufacturing
but also of management, Gildan has been able to achieve its aim of being the low-

est-cost producer in a cost-competitive market, while ensuring the highest worker rights, environmental and social standards are adhered to. Local staff have benefited greatly – which builds loyalty and commitment – furthering company objectives as well as the wider social good. 'This is a company that has supported us at every moment, at every level . . . everyone here is important to the company and we are respected' (Nubia Obando, Production Coordinator, Honduras).

Key to the responsible offshoring by Gildan has been a long-term commitment to working in the new manufacturing 'hubs'. Investments in training and education are long-term commitments, which pay dividends to those who can localise their operations successfully. The lesson here is that responsible outsourcing should both improve company performance and create local opportunities. By investing in education, Gildan sets the stage for future growth as well as developing a loyal and skilled workforce.

Sustained competitive advantage

Gildan has localised its manufacturing and operations in a way that uses CSR to build sustained competitive advantage. By placing the CSR agenda at the core of the business strategy of localisation, Gildan has successfully positioned itself for growth in a way that its competitors will find difficult to replicate. The company management correctly identified that 'sweatshops' of low-wage, low-skill workers were no longer acceptable to staff, consumers or the community and, as importantly, that unmotivated workers are not conducive to growing a business. Having recognised this, Gildan then built partnerships with NGOs and local communities, looking for ways to meet common objectives through cooperation. These relationships, and the trust inherent in them, are a source of advantage over Gildan's competitors. Most importantly, Gildan identified that having well-trained, motivated staff and managers was integral to achieving its aim of being the lowest-cost manufacturer in the market. To achieve this Gildan invested in training and rewarding staff, using CSR as a tool to build competitive advantage, creating local opportunities and contributing to the communities in which it works.

As a growing business, it is very much in Gildan's interests to grow and develop management talent, wherever in the world that talent is. With a focus on Central American and Caribbean production, Gildan has localised much of its management and operations to these 'hubs'. Creating these sorts of local opportunity has required long-term investment, especially in education and training, but these are business investments that pay dividends in the long run. This also builds local trust, making working in these countries much easier and less prone to shut-downs and industrial disputes. It will be difficult for other companies to try to replicate Gildan's model of achieving cost efficiencies through investment in CSR because of the long-term partnerships that are essential to making the strategy work. Some companies have tried to localise their operations in the same region. But they have met with only mixed success because they did not put CSR at the core of their localisation strategy. A corporate commitment to CSR is something that needs to be genuine and needs to come from the highest levels. Gildan clearly has this. The challenge is then in 'localising' CSR principles and practices into local operations and among the local management team.

What this case study demonstrates is how globalising operations, offshoring, need not be about reducing worker pay and conditions. Instead, by maintaining control of their operations, and building long-term relationships with suppliers, contractors, NGOs and communities, Gildan has demonstrated how CSR can be an investment that produces public good and improves private profit. Key to this strategy has been a commitment to use global operations to impact local communities, in a way that reduces overall company costs, while contributing to the communities in which the company operates.

Conclusion

Going local with your operations holds greater corporate responsibilities — and much greater corporate opportunities — than just offshoring or outsourcing. By moving business operations into low-cost markets, companies assume significant responsibilities. There is a responsibility to make a positive contribution to the local economy, to develop and train workers who may not have been in the formal workforce before and to demonstrate environmental stewardship, beyond minimum standards. These responsibilities are no longer negotiable, governments and consumers are increasingly aware of the local impacts of offshoring, companies need to be proactive to beat the competition.

Inherent in these responsibilities there are tremendous opportunities. By establishing operations in a developing country, by 'right-shoring' manufacturing and business services into countries with a comparative advantage, companies can save money and make a meaningful contribution to local development. As the Gildan case study illustrates so clearly, it is not a case of compromising business goals or profitability to achieve social responsibility or environmental protection. Rather, corporate success (and responsibility to shareholders) can combine with social responsibility (to stakeholders and the environment). By doing this better than other companies, Gildan has gained a long-term strategic advantage over its competitors.

The lesson from Gildan is that localising a business is about more than moving manufacturing offshore. In going *beyond offshoring*, Gildan has gone local not only with its production but also its core business management, maintenance, sales and HR management. To achieve this, training and education have been essential investments, which yield shared value for the company and for the community. This education and training has enabled Gildan to create *local opportunities* for staff, who have responded by being loyal and motivated, further helping to grow Gildan's business. This beneficial cycle of improved corporate and community growth is much more sustainable than simple outsourcing. It delivers sustained growth for the company and sustained cost reductions – while creating sustainable economic opportunities for the local community.

5

Evolution to revolution

Constant evolution and change is the key to meeting your responsibilities and taking advantage of the opportunities of CSR. At each step along the value chain, it is important to constantly seek new solutions to problems, new ways of producing the goods and services that you sell, in order to maximise the public good, minimise environmental impacts and maximise profit. This is crucial for companies serving the bottom of the pyramid, in reducing costs and making goods and services available to poor markets. It is equally crucial – and equally challenging – for companies working at the top of the pyramid, as the Scandic Hotels case study shows, for addressing their social and environmental responsibilities. Once the 'easy' CSR solutions have been taken, to constantly improve and tackle the problems unique to the 'hard' industries, innovation is essential.

Constant evolution builds on the previous three steps of CSR, leveraging your core competence, collaborating based on core values and taking your operations local wherever possible. Constant evolution is, first, about improving on your existing core competences, finding new ways to do what it is you already do well. The second step is then creating collaboration for change, drawing on the skills and resources of your partners to drive innovation. Third, these solutions must be localised, adapted to suit different markets and meet different consumer needs. Sometimes this process will be evolutionary, gradually improving on existing processes. Sometimes it will be revolutionary, such as Nokia moving from making rubber boots to making mobile phones (Hamel 2000), but in both instances it is achieved by a commitment to the core competence. In order to innovate, especially if you are entering new markets, collaboration is essential. Local partners contribute their CCs, they bring new ideas and new ways to do things that you can learn from to help you to constantly evolve and face new challenges.

Having built partnerships and gone local with core business operations, companies must constantly evolve, changing how their supply chain and business model operates. This occurs through step-by-step, incremental changes, of evolution. These evolutionary changes are about 'doing what you do now, better' and are well suited to addressing the responsibilities that a company faces. But, if companies are to take advantage of the opportunities of CSR, large-scale innovations, which change the way in which they do business, will also be required. These are revolutionary innovations, which affect the underlying business model. This does not mean abandoning your core competences; on the contrary, it requires you to take your core competences, apply them in new and challenging ways and to do this in concert with your local partners and stakeholders.

The idea that companies need to innovate is not new, nor is the suggestion that companies need to manage change to maintain their competitive advantage. What is new is the reason why companies need to do this. No longer is it acceptable to talk purely in terms of shareholder returns and stock market value. Rather, companies need to create value for society. Shareholders, owners and investors, remain at the centre of these concerns. But there are also wider responsibilities, and opportunities, that exist with stakeholders, society and in protecting the environment. Changing to meet these challenges requires: building on existing skills, managing evolution and encouraging revolution.

Building on existing skills

Within your current supply chain and company processes, you will already be having a series of impacts on society and the environment. These will include both positive and negative effects. The focus of CSR is on enhancing the positive and minimising the negative, creating competitive advantage for your company by doing this better than the competition. 'Cookie-cutter' CSR policies, such as listing which charities your company gives money to, without any strategic direction, do not create value for the company, nor do they necessarily enhance the public good. It is more important to look for the responsibilities and opportunities unique to your business. How you decide which issues are important for your business depends on your own shareholder and stakeholder priorities. Consulting with your stakeholders is an important part of this process. Building a 'hierarchy of social and environmental issues' as discussed in Chapter 2 (Table 1) helps you to identify the most important social and environmental impacts that you make. The question then is what to do with this information.

In some cases, existing solutions exist to help solve certain problems. Then it is a question of adapting this existing solution to meet your specific problem. But in many cases solutions do not exist; this is where companies need to compete to create new and different solutions to their problems. The ideal outcome of this is to move from a lose–lose situation to a win–win solution. So, if you are currently polluting the environment, this is harming the public good and may also be hurting your profits (either because of the cost of regulation/fines, or through lost brand value). It is in your interests to change. The ideal outcome is one that improves the public good (in this example improves the environment, perhaps by a proactive clean-up) as well as improves profitability (reduced business costs, enhanced brand value). But, if any known solution existed, you would use it. So, achieving a win–win will require a new solution. You will have to innovate.

Having identified the social or environmental impact that you want to address, a series of logical steps (laid out in Fig. 8) guides you through the process. First you need to see if the solution can be found within your existing core competences. If yes, then it is a case of using your CC to further enhance your competitive advantage. This gives you greater leverage over the competition; it builds the strength of your business and is the best case scenario. However, if your CC cannot be leveraged to address the issue, then this is where you need to use the capacities of collaborators. By working in concert with your stakeholders – customers, staff, suppliers and society – it is possible to take advantage of their unique skills, core competences and abilities, and to use these to build your business. Local partners, working in different markets (and the process of going local itself, see Chapter 4) will have their own abilities to create innovative solutions to your problems. The key is managing this process in a way that creates shared value. This is strategic CSR, leveraging your core competences and using the power of partnerships, and it can help address most social and environmental issues. But not all issues can be dealt with through evolution. This is where it is necessary to truly change the way you conduct business: to bring about a revolution.

Different problems will require different approaches. Sometimes you will need a blend of approaches to confront complex and interlocking challenges. Take, for instance, the case of Lifebuoy soap (see Fig. 9), often taken as an example of how companies can create shared value by targeting the 'bottom of the pyramid'. Hindustan Lever Limited (HLL), experiencing a drop in soap sales and aware of its obligation as a FMCG company working in India, decided to treat the

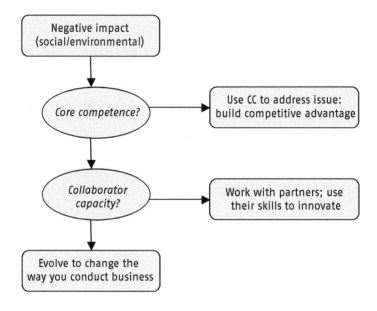

Figure 8 **Flow chart for evolution**

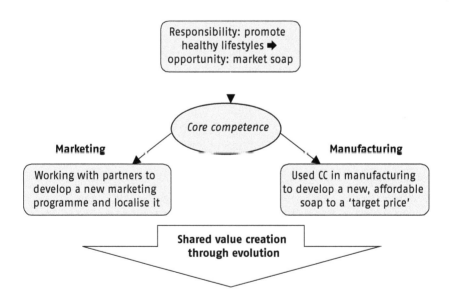

Figure 9 **HLL and evolution to create shared value**

fight against diarrhoeal diseases as an opportunity. The opportunity was 'to stim-ulate demand for soap through education campaigns'[52] which would help reduce the instance of diarrhoeal diseases in rural India, build sales and enhance the brand.

The first step was in recognising that HLL has an obligation to help contribute to social development in rural India, to make its products accessible to an under-served population, and that this presented an opportunity to create shared value. The second step was finding a way to serve this market, which required a much cheaper bar of soap than previously:

> Lifebuoy is priced to be affordable to the masses . . . Very often people in business you find people that do cost plus pricing . . . You have to start by saying I'm going to offer this benefit, let's say its germ kill. Let's say its Lifebuoy. You have to work out what people are going to pay. That's my price . . . that gives you your tar-get cost — or challenge cost. Then you have to create a business model that delivers that challenge cost (HLL Chairman Manvinder Singh Banga; in Prahalad 2004).

HLL has a core competence in processing consumer products on a mass scale, using research to improve its products and reduce environmental impacts. This CC was leveraged to create a milled soap (harder, giving better value for money) with added Triclosan (an antibacterial agent) to improve the health impact of hand washing. In this way HLL was able to create a new product which was acces-sible to the rural poor, for whom 9.50 rupees (approximately US$0.20) represents value for money, in reduced instances of disease and loss of work through illness.

The third step of marketing this soap was outside the core competence of HLL. While HLL has experience in marketing products to middle-income consumers, who are aware of the benefits of good hygiene, the company did not have the skills to target the rural poor. When it looked at creating the competence 'in-house', the cost would be too high to keep Lifebuoy at the 'target price'. This is where partnerships were created with an advertising agency, Ogilvy & Mather, which did have the CC and used this to work with local governments. Local facil-itators were hired to conduct training sessions in rural areas that educated peo-ple on the benefits of healthy hand washing. This step of localisation of the mar-keting chain reduced the cost of site visits from US$87 to US$17.[53] Further, by mobilising the resources of local and international development agencies, HLL was able to create a public–private partnership, which reinforced the marketing campaign and reduced the marketing cost.

By differentiating its product as a low-cost investment in good health, HLL cre-ated growth in Lifebuoy sales of 30%. The benefits in terms of improved health, reduced incidence of diarrhoeal disease and improved livelihoods is difficult to quantify but is certainly significant, evidenced both by the increased demand for the soap and by the willingness of local governments to participate in the programme. HLL has built its brand, improved profits and contributed to the public good – an excellent example of creating shared value.

However, HLL was not able to do this without changing how it operated; it was not able to do it alone. R&D within the company to create an affordable antibacterial soap leveraged HLL's core competences. This was an evolutionary form of innovation to solve a particular problem. To market this new product, collaboration was necessary, to make use of CCs that were outside of HLL's core business. Going local was important in driving innovation further, enabling HLL to meet its 'target price' and to respond quickly to market developments. This is a good example of how evolution along the value chain was central to creating shared value, enabling HLL to turn its corporate responsibility into an opportunity.

Managing evolution

To promote responsible change you need to invest. R&D requires laboratory funding, changing business processes entails short-term disruptions and future market creation requires investments: innovation costs money. But, as with any other business decision, failure to invest assures you only of reduced future returns. Investment in innovation for CSR is no different. Investment is required, but these investments need to pay returns in the long term. The challenge of investing in CSR is that the payoff is often very long-term, especially if you are investing in creating future markets at the bottom of the pyramid. This requires innovation to be managed in a way that encourages long-term investment, without losing sight of the current obligations to investors and short-term business needs. This is where an *evolutionary* approach is useful, encouraging constant evolution in how your business operates.

So, if a financial services firm decides to target the bottom of the pyramid, it is investing in creating a market for its services. With 3.7 billion people worldwide currently lacking access to financial services, this is a significant future market. But the decision to engage with these potential customers has to be driven primarily by a desire to create profits and shareholder value. In going after this profit, the responsible corporation then looks for ways to create shared value, finding opportunities to improve the public good through providing financial services. This shared value approach in turn expands the market and grows profits. But achieving this requires evolving the current business model to suit this new market.

In attempting to manage evolution, it is vital that the company has a clear *strategy* for its corporate social responsibility. CSR should contribute to the long-term strategic direction of the company and CSR spending needs to be seen as an investment, not a cost. Investments in CSR need to pay dividends, promoting and sustaining company growth as well as enhancing the public good. Managing towards this overall strategic direction requires engagement with the three main groups of stakeholders in the company: staff, consumers and suppliers.

Staff and strategic CSR

Your staff are crucial for innovation. How they do their jobs each day, their ability to change their working approach to suit new challenges and their inputs into building your strategic response to CSR, are all central to the success of innovation. The first step for a responsible company is to invest in its staff as engines of change, which drives the second step of utilising staff skills to develop the business. Traditional management textbooks talk about how staff improvement is inherent in continuous improvement, with examples such as the *Toyota Way* (Liker 2003) showing the benefits of engaging staff in innovation.

The first step, investing in staff, is not only responsible behaviour; it is good HR and sound management. The key is to make these investments ones that build a more qualified, motivated and adaptable workforce to bolster company performance and innovation efforts. This is where training is essential. In many cases government help is available to companies wishing to make these sorts of long-term investment in staff. Schemes such as the UK's 'Investor in People' award and the EU's 'Life Long Learning' initiative can help fund company investments in staff. Some company CSR policies, such as encouraging volunteering, fit well into this sort of 'soft' investment, producing strategic CSR outcomes as well as improving staff capabilities, loyalty and goodwill. For instance, TNT has contributed staff volunteer time to WFP's disaster relief efforts (see Table 2). Time spent volunteering is often discussed by staff as crucial learning exercises for their work. In applying this model to your business it is important that the volunteering is linked to leveraging and building company core competences. This ensures that the recipient charity gains the maximum benefit and it ensures that your company profits.

The second step in encouraging innovation is utilising the potential of your staff to identify, target and obtain the *opportunities* of strategic CSR. Often staff, who work closely with consumers, suppliers and society, are aware of opportunities that exist for CSR. Likewise, as stakeholders they have an interest in ensuring the success of the CSR strategy. To take advantage of these opportunities, *participation* is vital. Staff must be part of CSR strategy development, their inputs into how the company can evolve are crucial, and their understanding of the needs of other stakeholders is priceless. This is why developing the CSR strategy should be an open process. While the initial decision to become a responsible company is one taken at the top, all staff should be involved in formulating the CSR strategy. Their knowledge should be accessed to innovate and improve the CSR strategy once it is in place. In this way the potential of staff as your most important knowledge assets can be tapped and used to create shared value.

Adding voice to choice

Engaging with consumers is a powerful tool to enable your company to evolve. If you want to be quick in your response to consumer demand, it pays to communicate. Listen to customers and engage with them in explaining your CSR strategy. Understanding evolving customer demands enables companies to serve their needs better. Responding more quickly to new market opportunities and seeing the opportunities inherent in considering consumers as partners can create competitive advantage. CSR is an excellent way to do this, through strategic innovation.

In the consumer goods industries (food, clothing, etc.) companies have come under increased pressure in recent years to deal with their environmental and social impacts. Companies that identified these risks early on have been able to turn responsibility into opportunity, by bringing new goods to market that meet consumer demand. Perhaps the most famous instance is fair-trade coffee, in all its guises (and despite some questions about its usefulness for development), which shows how consumer choice is driving the market (see Box 4).

Proactive companies have the chance to 'give voice to choice' by working with consumers on issues that concern them. British Airways, aware of consumer concern about the contribution of air travel to global warming, runs such a scheme. By allowing customers to calculate their CO_2 emissions, BA is contributing to awareness of the issue. For instance a return flight from London to Singapore contributes 2.46 tonnes of CO_2 to the atmosphere.[54] Customers can then choose to buy carbon offsets of US$33.32, funding projects ranging from community lighting in South Africa, energy-efficient lamps for schools in Kazakhstan to bio-fuel school stoves in India, for only a small proportion of the US$1,300 cost of such a flight. Not a bad price to pay to assuage your conscience when jet-setting has been described as the new 'farting loudly' (*The Economist* 2007b).

Non-consumer goods companies often find it more difficult to identify such opportunities for quick and effective engagement with their customers. However, as understanding of supply chains increases, suppliers are coming under increasing scrutiny. Twenty years ago few people would know that their clothes were made with child labour; now many consumers are active in demanding fair labour sources. Yet today few people are aware of the labour (including forced and child labour) that goes into *growing* cotton; a proactive company will identify this issue and work with consumers to see the opportunity in this risk. Equally, business-to-business corporate responsibility is becoming increasingly important; companies are actively seeking eco-labelled and fair-trade assured supplies of everything from hotel rooms, to coffee to printer cartridges. This is where supply chains are increasingly important for strategic CSR as a way of leveraging company strategy.

Man is born free: but everywhere he is in supply chains

Engaging with suppliers, and wider society, also helps businesses to meet their corporate responsibilities. By taking a supply chain approach, companies can analyse their *responsibilities* and *opportunities* at every step of the business process. This sometimes leads to surprising results and novel opportunities.

The supply chain approach to business innovation has led to activities such as building small businesses in countries such as Azerbaijan, where the oil riches are not evenly distributed. To help develop local communities, and to manage political risk, BP and Shell have decided to 'buy local' for some of their equipment, such as fireproof gloves, which are sown at home by women. This reduces the companies' overall business costs, localising their supply chains in a way that also feeds money back into the communities in which they work. In the same way South African mining firms provide free antiretroviral drugs and HIV testing for employees, both to reduce their costs and to be seen to be 'contributing' to society. This helps reduce the 'risk' to companies operating in uncertain political environments and improves their 'licence to operate'.

Yet incremental action is not always enough. In many cases in the developing world, the extractive industries (mining, oil) are engaged largely because of political pressure. This pressure is both domestic and a result of awareness building in the developed world. At a global level, the engagement of major companies in carbon trading schemes must be seen as a result of public and governmental pressure rather than altruism. This is fine; it is businesses responding to public pressure in a proactive manner, appropriate for operating in a democracy. Applying these lessons to innovation along the supply chain means that the human and environmental costs of each step of business activity need to be properly accounted for; purely financial measures fail to do this. 'Triple bottom line' and 'total cost' accounting systems can be useful processes through which businesses identify the risks and opportunities of their own value chain, but environmental pricing is also an essential element of this to avoid the 'free-rider' dilemma.

With growing global supply chains, stretching from the farm gate to urban marketplace, there is real potential for partnerships. Yet to date few firms have had the courage, or political prompting, to apply CSR to their entire supply chain

Box 4 **Thought provoker: fair trade and fairy tales?**

One often-cited example of how the private sector can be utilised to promote social development is that of fair trade. Initially promoted by the non-governmental community, fair trade has been adopted (or co-opted) by international businesses. The concept behind fair trade is that consumers pay a premium price to ensure that the producers of their products receive a 'fair' price. This has been especially effective in the coffee market, where numerous small farmers are largely at the whim of international coffee futures — traded on the Chicago Board of Trade — which has a considerable impact on their livelihoods yet is something over which they have no control. This volatility in price also makes it difficult for smallholders to invest in their future crops. Fair-trade coffee has enabled large numbers of coffee smallholders, especially in Latin America (though notably not in Vietnam and other 'controlled' economies), to develop their communities through economic growth.

The provision of 'fair price', and more recently 'ethical-trade' and 'equitrade', coffee products is now big business. Worldwide sales of fair trade-certified coffee in 2007 were worth US$87 million. But this is still only a tiny fraction of the overall world coffee trade, worth US$10 billion annually. Big business is also in on the act: for example, Starbucks, the Seattle-based coffee-bar chain, has introduced 'premium' brand coffee in some of its outlets. Most European supermarkets also use the fair-trade label as a way of distinguishing 'premium' products for 'ethical' consumers. Yet fair trade is not without its problems. For instance, a scandal in September 2006 centred on several different 'certification organisations' whose 'fair-trade' coffee from Peru was picked by workers receiving under the national minimum wage. This can be seen as an anomaly; coffee supply chains are long (although other products such as cotton are much more complex) and certification organisations are short on resources. However, it does point to several problems with the fair-trade approach, including a lack of shared standards, its voluntary nature and the preference that fair trade has for direct consumer goods (coffee, cocoa beans) over non-consumer direct products (such as cotton, often processed in a country different from that of origin).

By seeing fair trade as a premium product, for which a multitude of different standards exist, fair trade risks becoming misleading. Labels range from 'bird-friendly' (surrounding trees are not to be cut down),

continued opposite →

'organic' (a change-over that takes roughly five years), to 'ethical' (any number of meanings) and there are numerous different labels calling themselves 'fair trade'. Surely it would be better to establish global minimum standards for agricultural production, and to hold companies to account for all their products? By persisting as seeing fair trade as a premium product, rather than a basic minimum, the majority of coffee producers are disenfranchised. It is necessary for business, governments and civil society to come together and establish global minimum standards for labour and environmental impact of agriculture. Certification organisations would still have a role to play, but businesses – with their advanced supply chain management expertise – could be held to legal account for *all* their produce, not just for a lucky elite of consumer-driven products.

(see Box 4). Opportunities exist in business development, supply chain management and finance, areas in which businesses are traditionally strong and the government and NGO community are weak. So, just as supply chains were localised for safety equipment in Azerbaijan, so too can firms build small enterprises in poor areas which promote employment, by leveraging their core competences. This can benefit business, through the promotion of better 'farm gate' quality controls or by encouraging fair-trade-style direct marketing, all of which private enterprise can contribute to and benefit from. The key lesson is that evolution along every step of the supply chain needs to be part of a company's strategic approach to CSR.

Encouraging revolution

Not all of your corporate responsibilities will be addressed by incremental changes in your supply chain. Evolution can address most issues, but some persistent problems require a reorientation in your business. This means moving away from 'doing what you do now – better' towards 'changing what you do'. This concept of a revolution, of radical innovation, can be seen as an opportunity to create strategic advantage through corporate responsibility. For some corporate responsibilities, a total reorientation in how we do business is perhaps necessary. For some industries, whose work is inherently polluting, there is a choice here between becoming the 'best in class' and minimising these impacts through evolution and substantively altering how they work, through revolution.

In the case of climate change we need a change in incentives, encouraging carbon reduction by making it profitable to find alternatives; this is an evolution of existing environmental regulation. But, to combat global hunger, a realignment of corporate goals is required and, while governments play a role, companies must also take a lead in encouraging revolution. Revolution is necessary when you can't match your *responsibilities* with your *capabilities* to meet these obligations. Revolution is only necessary when there are no *opportunities* for evolutionary change. When this is the case then revolution is essential.

In *Leading the Revolution* Gary Hamel (2000) argues that radical innovations are essential to maintaining a competitive advantage. In confronting 'non-linear' challenges, corporations need to find 'non-linear' solutions. He argues that the challenges of business today are so different from those in the past; old solutions are leading to '*rising expectations and diminishing returns*'. This same argument can be used for corporate social responsibility. The traditional responsibilities facing business (site pollution, employment) are currently being addressed, so companies need to be strategic in seeking out new ways to derive competitive advantage. Conversely, climate change is probably the first issue that threatens the basis of the global economy, calling into doubt the ability of business to continue. This is one case, among many, where these new *responsibilities* and *challenges* cannot be addressed by business as usual. This is why companies need to experiment with revolutionary change to try to create new opportunities.

But it would be wrong to always seek revolution. Most problems, for most companies, can be solved through evolution. When we are seeking to create shared value this change can often occur incrementally: a constant evolution that eventually leads to revolutionary results, without taking the massive risks of revolution. The end goal is a 100% sustainable supply chain, but steps towards this are just as valuable as the end goal. In encouraging revolution we should be mindful that today's revolutionary hero can be tomorrow's tyrant. One of the 'gray-haired revolutionaries' of Hamel's work was Enron, which illustrates the risks of revolution if it is not carried out in a responsible manner. So, while companies should try to be revolutionary in how they conduct business, this must be responsible revolution, with awareness of their obligations to shareholders, stakeholders, society and the environment.

Implementing this sort of revolution is notoriously difficult, especially in the 'hard' industries where many business activities are inherently polluting. The extractive industries have made considerable gains in the past 10–15 years, as the earlier chapters illustrate, in improving their value creation for society. The case study of Scandic, below, shows how one firm, working in the 'hard' sector of hospitality, has revolutionised its social and environmental performance. But this revolution has been achieved through engagement with society, outside partners and staff — all focused on the concept of *Omtanke* (Swedish for 'care and consideration').

Case study: Scandic hotels and *Omtanke*

In 1991 Scandic, a hotel chain based in Scandinavia, was almost bankrupt. Poor economic conditions, high staffing costs and competition were squeezing the profit margins of this mid-market hotel chain. A bold decision was made by a new CEO, Roland Nilsson, to pursue environmental sustainability as a core business principle. The drive behind this was an attempt to create a customer relationship based on common values, to build a brand for Scandic that created value for shareholders and stakeholders. As Jan Peter Bergkvist[55] points out:

> We are a people business. Our products, sales and pricing can be copied by our competitors, quickly, in real time with the internet. Our concepts and methods are more difficult to copy, but our competition can still copy these in, say, four months. What they cannot copy is our customer relationships, our values. These are based on shared values, on a sustainable brand, built on environmentally and socially sustainable business practices and environmental protection.

Building a sustainable brand, and gaining competitive advantage over other mid-market hotels, was possible only by innovating at every step along the supply chain and by placing environmental sustainability at the core of the business. As Figure 10 shows, at every step up the value chain, from product and price towards customer relationships and values, the degree of difficulty increases. This takes time, it takes commitment from the highest levels of the company and it takes a commitment to constant evolution.

Working towards a goal of a sustainable brand involved suppliers, team members (staff) and sustained commitment from the management. To do this Scandic placed *Omtanke* at the centre of the business model. The concept of *Omtanke*, Swedish for 'care and consideration', involves a service mentality about 'how we serve our guests and each other'. *Omtanke* is at the heart of the 'Compass Programme', which incorporates economic, ethical and ecological principles, shown in Figure 11. Every Scandic business decision is reflected in these three business concepts: economic concerns drive ethical considerations and ecological choices, which in turn drive economic growth.

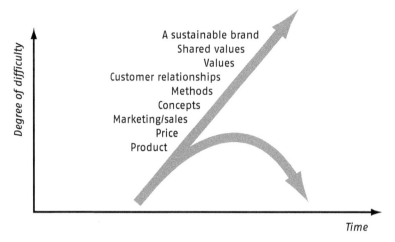

Figure 10 **Creating a sustainable brand**

Source: Courtesy of Scandic Hotels 2007

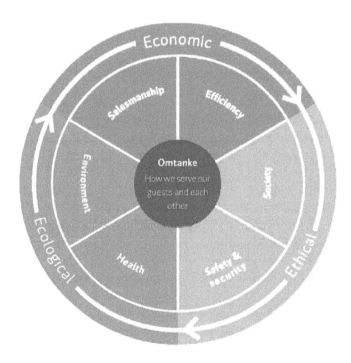

Figure 11 **Scandic's Compass Programme**

Source: Courtesy of Scandic Hotels 2007

The results of placing *Omtanke* and environmental sustainability at the core of the business have been impressive. Scandic is now the biggest hotel in the Nordic market, with 130 hotels in nine countries and 5,700 team members. Scandic enjoys significant competitive and profit advantage over other chains, because of its customer loyalty, brand value and improved cost structure. Moreover, it is a symbol of how the travel industry can make a contribution to building a sustainable society.

To achieve this Scandic took several steps that were crucial. It decided on a core competence early on and built it, training staff and investing in stakeholder involvement. It then collaborated with advisers and labelling organisations to extend its brand value. This was followed by constant evolution along the supply chain, adding value and reducing environmental cost wherever possible.

Omtanke as a core competence

Concern for customers and the environment is described by Scandic as 'Nordic common sense'. Looking after clients, staff, the environment and contributing to social development is crucial to how Scandic does business. As a hotel chain, the company realises that, if people feel unsafe or live in unhealthy environments, the business will ultimately fail. The ability to meet customer needs by showing care and consultation is a core competence for Scandic. As a holistic approach to business, encompassing staff training, customer relationships and supply chain management, it provides competitive advantage. Other hotels cannot easily copy it, and, so long as Scandic continues to innovate, it will continue to have an advantage over the competition.

Scandic recognises that to provide the *Omtanke* customer experience, good staff are crucial. All training starts with the 5,700 'team members', who are engaged in a 'dialogue' in the four areas of safety, Scandic values, sales and service, and environmental sustainability. New ideas from staff are welcome in helping to innovate along the value chain, and these innovations are shared throughout the hotel chain through an intranet site. The focus of the training is on *enabling* people to make the 'right' decisions.

Encouraging behaviour change takes an investment in team training, but it is one that pays dividends. A 1996 initiative to promote energy-efficient behaviours reduced energy costs by 24%, a training investment that was paid off in six months. To review this, staff performance is assessed annually using the 'Get Smart' review, encompassing the four objectives of *Omtanke*, economics, ethics and ecology. Besides reducing business costs, this focus on staff training builds the Scandic brand as eco-friendly and enhances the customer experience.

As part of the service industry, how Scandic treats its guests is part of its core competence. The *Omtanke* approach is one of concern for guests, listening to their concerns and addressing their needs. Part of this is informing guests, making them aware of the ecological impact of their activities and giving them the choice to change their behaviour. 'We believe, almost religiously, that people want to be sustainable. If you give people the information they will act sustainably. It is that simple and that complex.'[56]

These choices range from letting guests choose whether to re-use their towels (Scandic was one of the first companies in the industry to take this, now common, initiative) to encouraging waste sorting. This has helped reduce unsorted waste from 1.5 to 0.5 kg per guest per night. Scandic has also been proactive in consulting with customers, especially business clients, in determining their priorities for environmental protection. This has led to new initiatives, such as the 'Scandic Shop', allowing for the replacement of energy-inefficient mini-bars with a more sociable, environmentally friendly option for guests.

The Natural Step and Nordic Swan

> We are not environmental experts. We want to do the right thing,
> but we need a partner to help us understand how to do this.[57]

Achieving environmental sustainability requires expertise outside of the core competence of a hotel. This is where Scandic realised the need to create strategic partnerships with advisers The Natural Step and the eco-labelling organisation Nordic Swan. Both of these partnerships were forged on the idea of creating shared value for both organisations; each company contributed its core competence towards the goal of environmental sustainability.

The Natural Step (TNS), an advisory NGO that applies a scientific and rigorous approach to sustainable development, was engaged from the outset. TNS brought its systematic approach to CSR, its expertise in implementing change within companies and its framework for consistent environmental management to the partnership. This engagement with The Natural Step was founded at the highest levels; Scandic's CEO and 100 senior managers went on a five-day retreat in 1994, one full day of which was with the founder of TNS. This sort of early engagement, from the initial stages of the project, quickly worked its way through Scandic's team. Within one year of this workshop, all 5,000 Scandic team members had received TNS training, and over 1,500 operational suggestions had not only been put forward by staff, but actually been implemented (Nattrass and Altomare 2007). Today, this training has been internalised into the *Omtanke* programme and all new team members are trained in the TNS approach.

It was the introduction of this TNS 'framework' that enabled Scandic to move beyond good intentions and into action. By focusing on a systems approach to pollution, environmental initiatives were introduced in a way that took account of the entire supply chain, looking for opportunities for innovation and engaging team members in this 'journey'.[58] This approach also ensures that Scandic, with TNS in partnership, continues to innovate and find new solutions to persistent environmental problems. It is very much a partnership based on trust, long-term commitment from both parties and periodically re-examining existing processes to find new solutions.

The Nordic Swan eco-label was initially established by the Nordic council of ministers as the pre-eminent environmental sustainability label. As a standard that improves every three years, with a membership cost of 0.15% of turnover, this is not an easy or cheap partnership for Scandic to engage in. But it is one that helps to build the Scandic brand and is part of the company's wider corporate responsibility. The fact that Scandic Sweden became the first eco-labelled hotel chain in the world in 2004 and now has 92 eco-labelled hotels shows how important this partnership is for Scandic's success in the CSR field. Scandic has contributed to improving the Nordic Swan standards, and has participated in creating 'EcoRoom' standards and in sharing these lessons with other hotel companies under the International Tourism Partnership umbrella for hotels operating in the developing world.[59]

Innovation and new initiatives

By choosing to lead the industry, Scandic did not have 'ready-made' solutions to the environmental sustainability challenges it faced. The company had to develop new initiatives. This required a constant evolution in business practices, changing its relationships with suppliers and altering the value chain to create shared value. It is precisely these *business processes* that are difficult for competitors to copy and that form the basis of Scandic's sustainable brand. But this is a never-ending challenge, the end goal is to have a perfectly sustainable hotel, which is still a long way away and will require continued innovation.

Some changes that Scandic made early on, such as providing a choice to replace or re-use towels, have been taken up elsewhere in the industry. Interestingly, many of the most visible innovations – such as encouraging guests to use less electricity – have more of an awareness raising than a substantive impact (Taylor 2006). The greatest improvements come from systematic changes: installing eco-labelled light bulbs and moving towards safe chemicals for cleaning, as well as installing in-room sorting bins. Each of these innovations is driven by a desire to improve the three segments of the compass programme: economics, ethics and the environment. Changes in business processes and the supply chain must meet these three criteria, which together constitute a journey towards a sustainable business and brand.

Environment and the EcoRoom

Scandic's environmental policy (1994):

> No company can avoid taking responsibility for the environment and focusing on environmental issues.
>
> Scandic shall, therefore, lead the way and work continuously to promote both a reduction in our environmental impact and a better environment.
>
> Scandic shall contribute to a sustainable society.

The hotel industry is a micro-society in focus; the same impacts that human behaviour has on the environment are focused within the hospitality industry. Energy use, transportation, water consumption, chemicals, fixtures and fittings and waste all contribute to environmental degradation. Scandic decided to focus on these six environmental issues, addressing the impacts of its business operations, through the Nordic Swan certification process. Initiatives have included a business-wide 'ban' on giant shrimps, an icon of unsustainable fisheries, which was not even identified as an environmental issue ten years ago. This is the point of constant evolution; it is about always pushing the limits and experimenting with new solutions. As new issues emerge, new solutions will be required, providing new opportunities to create shared value. Taking this evolutionary approach, Scandic has attempted to deal with environmental issues in a holistic manner, especially through the 'EcoRoom' concept, pioneered in 1994.

The EcoRoom concept is a life-cycle approach to building hotel rooms. It is about improving guest satisfaction and reducing business cost by designing functional, eco-friendly hotel rooms. By using locally sourced wood, wool and cotton, EcoRooms are 97% recyclable, more durable (reducing maintenance costs), easier to clean (important with a US$30 per hour labour cost) and energy-conserving (important with the Nordic winter). Scandic has built 11,000 Eco-Rooms, helping reduce their energy and cleaning costs, creating shared value for guests and the company, while reducing the ecological footprint of guest visits. Functional Nordic design has added to Scandic's core competence of *Omtanke*, improving the customer experience and creating competitive advantage.

Social sustainability and inclusion

Health, inclusion and safety were identified by Scandic as both responsibilities and opportunities for its business. Contributing to healthy lifestyles and communities is an important obligation for Nordic companies; communities expect it and staff compete to work for responsible employers. Scandic set the goal of being the healthiest company in the hospitality sector, by promoting healthy choices. This took innovative forms: for example, some hotels offer morning runs with the hotel manager as a way to promote healthy choices among guests and staff.

Safety for guests and staff was another area where Scandic's social responsibilities grew beyond what might have been initially envisaged. Taking the view that 'no guest or staff member's safety must be put at risk' Scandic built business processes to assure safety in all circumstances. Here again it led the industry, requiring room key cards to access elevators, keeping unwanted guests away from accommodation floors.

Inclusion was another issue that 'evolved' into the responsibility agenda. Following a team member's experience with a debilitating illness, Scandic recognised a responsibility to provide inclusion and access to disabled guests. In doing this, they also recognised a huge opportunity; with 1 million disabled people in Sweden alone (and 50 million across Europe) this is a large, and under-served, market opportunity. By providing wheelchair access, hearing aid loops, cup holders, and by training staff in disability assistance, Scandic added 15,000 new room bookings. This has grown into a partnership with the Swedish and Finnish Paralympic teams, further enhancing the Scandic brand and developing this specialised, but crucial, market.

Supply chains, linen and organic breakfasts

Scandic looked beyond 'end of pipe' pollution early on, adopting a holistic view of its environmental impact. In analysing and mitigating environmental impacts, Scandic adopted the *collaboration* approach to its supply chain. By looking for common solutions to common problems, suppliers and staff were engaged in the evolution of the supply chain and efforts to reduce the environmental impact. This step-by-step approach identified issues such as the outsourced laundry using an artificial whitener for the linen. Scandic decided that this was creating neither company nor community value and discontinued its use.

As early as 1995 Scandic stopped supplying individual toiletries in room, providing instead a qualitative dispenser of eco-friendly packaged soap and shampoo. Lux is a major supplier of these toiletries, and Scandic worked in partnership with it and Nordic Swan to change the global recipe of the Lux product to conform with eco-standards. This supply chain evolution had flow-on effects well beyond Scandic's own ecological footprint. A similar approach of partnership and evolution was taken in deciding to serve an organic breakfast buffet, in collaboration with the KRAV certifying agency in Sweden. Working in partnership with its coffee supplier, Scandic was able to initially shift to organic coffee at no extra cost, and more recently to fair-trade coffee for only US$60,000 extra per year. Guest satisfaction with the breakfast, as a healthy and nutritious choice, is driving increased return stays and contributing to business growth.

These are all just small examples, of the many, of how Scandic has used evolution along the supply chain to create shared value. By working with staff, training them and investing in their capacities, new solutions have evolved to difficult problems. Stakeholders, including guests and communities, have also been involved, and the way in which Scandic communicates with these stakeholders is part of its competitive advantage. Suppliers have been seen as partners, alongside external advisers and labelling organisations, in innovating to improve sustainability and reduce environmental impacts. This has created new opportunities: for instance, working with suppliers to move from using fossil-based plastics to organic plastics. Together, these lessons are useful for understanding how evolution along the value chain can create shared value.

Conclusions

Constant evolution drives competitive advantage. Innovating to improve your company's response to its corporate responsibilities enables you to create new corporate opportunities, building your brand and creating shared value for shareholders and society. But, to manage evolution successfully, several key steps are necessary.

First, you need to reorient the business towards economic, environmental and social sustainability. This leadership is required from the top, from the start. Scandic could not have evolved were it not for the almost revolutionary approach of the new CEO in pursuing a sustainable brand strategy. There needs to be a genuine commitment to engaging with problems and to solving these problems through an investment in innovation. Yet this sort of bold business is exactly the sort of leadership needed to create shared value for the company and society.

Having decided on this goal, leverage your core competences to innovate. Do what you already do well, better, and more sustainably. Find new ways of meeting customer demand and adapt your business processes in a way that your competitors cannot easily copy. In doing this you further develop your core competences and you can derive competitive advantage from this.

For problems that cannot be solved internally, collaborate. As with Scandic partnering with Nordic Swan and The Natural Step, so too can your company benefit from collaboration. Be sure to approach these strategically, aiming to create common value for the partners, on the basis of shared values and ideas.

Finally, apply this approach to every step of your supply chain. Work with staff; empower them to have an input into the innovation process, alongside suppliers, society, customers and the communities in which you work. It is only through the constant process of evolving your business model that you can sustain competitive advantage and brand value. But, in doing this, you are creating shareholder value that cannot easily be copied by your competitors, which also builds shared value for society.

6

Governments and the changing business climate

Tackling climate change and global inequality is not only the responsibility of business. Governments also have responsibility for these issues, which has traditionally been fulfilled through official development assistance and environmental regulation. The state plays an important role in setting the 'business climate' in which companies operate. This is the institutional setting, 'the rules of the game' under which business is conducted.[60] In promoting corporate social responsibility, good governments need to adopt a proactive approach to business, working collectively with companies to address problems that are too big or too complex to be dealt with alone. This is not to remove governments from their important role as regulators and enforcers of the rule of law; instead, it is to promote achieving these goals through a cooperative rather than adversarial approach.

The biggest contribution that the state can make is in setting the institutions, incentives and 'rules of the game' for companies to behave responsibly. This should start from recognising a market failure in how firms are encouraged to focus on short-term profitability (by the financial markets) at the expense of long-term planning, by improving the incentives for social and environmental investment. Likewise, the environmental impact of business is often increased by market failures that encourage firms to 'externalise' their pollution costs. This occurs because of an unnecessarily adversarial approach to environmental policy formulation, which prevents innovation and the development of constantly improving standards. The role of the state is in creating incentives and enforcing rules, not in mandating specific CSR policy. If we get the incentives right, firms will compete to comply, because it is in their financial interests to do so. This leaves businesses to focus on what they do best, creating jobs, innovating and generating wealth. Governments can shape the incentive structure to encourage shared value creation.

It is insufficient to leave social and environmental problems to the private sector and CSR. There is and always will be a role for governments. The question is how should governments fulfil their obligations and responsibilities, encouraging companies to seize the opportunities of CSR. If companies are engaged by governments, provided with the right incentives to promote social development and environmental protection, and are encouraged to do so in a way that presents a good business strategy, then there is real potential.

I identify here three main policy shifts which together can promote private-led social development and environmental protection. First governments need to seek to work with, rather than against, businesses. There has always been a privileged place of business in societies, which has sometimes led to collusion between the state and businesses. The response to this has been an adversarial approach between governments and the private sector, which is unhelpful for promoting CSR. This is why I advocate a cooperative rather than a coercive approach. Second, governments need to create tax and accounting incentives to specifically encourage corporate responsibility, taking account for the public good that 'spills over' from corporate responsibility — attributing economic value to the social value built by responsible companies. This is linked with the third policy shift, a move towards 'total cost accounting' of production which rewards, and punishes, firms on the basis of their impact on local communities and the environment.

Cooperation or coercion?

Governments set the rules, they are responsible to society to an extent that companies will never be, and they retain democratic legitimacy. Because of this, it is crucial that governments play a role in promoting corporate social responsibility. The traditional way of regulating businesses has been adversarial, taking a deliberately distant stance to avoid any allegations of collusion. There is no question that, for some forms of regulation (monopolies, criminal behaviour, etc.), this is appropriate. But, for promoting CSR, for managing social and environmental impacts and for encouraging social investment, cooperation is much more useful than coercion.

'Flexible' regulation, which is worked out between businesses and government, is often much more readily enforced, the costs to business and society reduced, and compliance tends to be higher. This does not mean that the regulations are 'softer' than traditional rules; in fact, they are often more effective. The crucial difference is that, by engaging with businesses, costs can be reduced and compliance increased. Take for example the regulation of the London and New York stock exchanges. The flexible regulatory approach of the LSE has been better at preventing market abuses and has enabled much more preparation for terrorist attacks (including full-scale simulations). The reason for this is that, by engaging with businesses, the regulator has the ability to harness private-sector abilities and to find 'middle-path' solutions that reduce regulation and compliance costs. In contrast, the United States Environmental Protection Agency (EPA) is often criticised for its adversarial approach. This ironically results in *lower* environmental standards, because of non-compliance and legislative interference at the behest of business interests.

Flexible regulation

Government regulations are only as effective as their implementation. The responsible corporation will comply with government rules, respecting its obligations to the countries in which it works. But in many cases *how* these regulations are implemented leads to very different results. Businesses can ultimately find ways around most regulations, sometimes resulting in unforeseen impacts, and encouraging a 'race to the bottom' towards unregulated countries. The best option for governments is to actively *consult* with businesses to find the best way to meet common goals and shared responsibilities. In some cases voluntary approaches may work, but in most cases compulsory standards will still be necessary, in order to avoid the 'free-rider' problem.

This is where a *policy process* (see Fig. 12) is needed whereby governments and businesses establish the social and environmental issues they wish to prioritise and regulate. An important part of this is weighing the cost–benefit ratio of regulation. This is where the environmental costs and benefits of a policy are put in monetary terms and the solution that creates the most public good, at the lowest cost, is chosen. The flexible approach is an excellent way to minimise costs and enhance benefits, as it allows businesses to innovate to create new solutions to environmental problems.

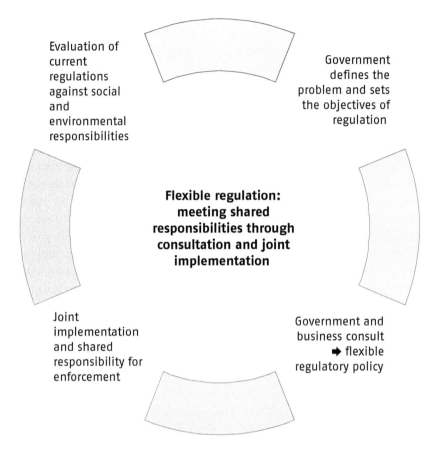

Evaluation of current regulations against social and environmental responsibilities

Government defines the problem and sets the objectives of regulation

Flexible regulation: meeting shared responsibilities through consultation and joint implementation

Joint implementation and shared responsibility for enforcement

Government and business consult ➡ flexible regulatory policy

Figure 12 **Process of flexible regulation**

In setting the environmental agenda, governments should consult with businesses to find the best way to address the issue, deciding on common standards and best practices. This involves searching for 'win–win' solutions and determining what sorts of cost society and businesses are prepared to pay. This is followed by joint implementation and shared responsibility for enforcement, creating a situation where companies compete to meet and exceed the regulations, rather than avoid them. Finally, the policy needs to be evaluated and adapted on a regular basis, continuing the process of flexible and responsive regulation.

The case study about Norwegian electrical goods pollution in this chapter provides a good example of how flexible environmental policy has been effective in promoting public good and private profit – encouraging shared value creation. The central issue to remember is that neither governments nor business can fulfil all their responsibilities alone. They need to cooperate, and in doing so they leverage their specific competences to arrive at superior outcomes. This requires governments to take the lead, but support and collaboration is also required from the private sector, which may involve breaking down some 'barriers' to collaboration and establishing new partnerships. Governments, civil society and business all have a role to play in creating shared value.

Doing business with bureaucrats

If you are in business and reading this, you might be wondering what you can do to work with governments. The answer, gladly, is a great deal. Doing business with bureaucrats is surprisingly like doing business with anyone else. Relationships matter, trust is important and any deal has to be based on common interests. If you apply the same rules you apply when entering into business partnerships, you are on the right track. The big difference is that, unlike businesses, governments don't measure their success by profits. This means that your counterparts in the public sector are driven by some very different performance indicators from those you are used to. They have targets, often non-financial, but still quantifiable, and their promotion is based on meeting these targets. But this doesn't mean you don't have shared interests and can't create shared value. On the contrary, doing business with bureaucrats can be profitable for both parties.

If you are doing business in a foreign country, especially if it is a poor nation, your home government's embassy can be a useful starting point. Diplomats, such as the economic attaché, are specifically charged with promoting economic interests and are often very approachable. If you are looking at creating a partnership with a local NGO, they might even be able to finance part of the investment through their development assistance budget. Multilateral institutions, such as the World Bank and the International Finance Corporation (IFC), are focused on promoting private-sector development; they typically speak the same 'language' of business and can be a useful source of co-financing for projects. For example, the IFC provided half of the initial funding in the Montana/AMAC example in Chapter 3.

The same is true in your host country: government agencies have targets for social development and environmental protection. If you can help them meet these targets, while conducting your business, then you are creating shared value. Often funding will be available, to reduce the costs of partnerships you establish and to help you manage the risk of seeking out new corporate opportunities. The key is in building up personal relationships and trust, as with any other business venture, and in looking for ways in which your cooperation can create shared value.

Encouraging responsible investment

Managers and directors are legally responsible to their investors. It is essential that business decisions are driven, primarily, by the desire to increase shareholder returns. This is crucial, as shareholders are the core responsibility of business. However, they are not the only responsibility; other stakeholders, society and the natural environment are also important. The circles of influence and responsibility in Chapter 1 help us to understand these responsibilities. In the normal pursuit of business, these responsibilities are complementary; creating shareholder returns also creates public good as we saw with the discussion of Adam Smith. The problem sometimes comes when, in the pursuit of increased investor returns, the public good or the environment is harmed. I would argue that in the long term this is bad for shareholder returns, as it risks reducing the market and damaging the company's brand. This is irresponsible investment, as it is not taking into account the long-term obligations of the business towards either its shareholders or the wider stakeholder community. This is why governments regulate, to ensure that public aims are met (or not damaged) in the pursuit of private profit. But this does not mean that profit should be seen as being *against* the public good.

Playing FTSE with corporate social responsibility

The challenge is to move towards a situation where the pursuit of private profit also leads to public gain, and that long-term investments in social development and environmental protection are recognised as sound investments. This move towards responsible investment is already happening: leading investment firms offer 'ethical investments' as a differentiated product to discerning customers. In the UK there are over 60 ethical funds, with over £6,000 million invested in them.[61] This interest has been recognised by the FTSE4Good index, which charts and facilitates investment in companies that meet global corporate responsibility criteria. Interestingly, the FTSE4Good index has outperformed the FTSE100 over the past five years, strengthening the argument that responsibility towards stakeholders is in the long-term interests of shareholders and investors as well.

The role of government in encouraging responsible investment is to ensure that the rules of the market encourage responsible investment and discourage the pursuit of private profit at the expense of society and the environment. This can be achieved through facilitation and regulation that encourages firms to create shared value for society.

Facilitation

The market, by itself, will not always come to the most responsible outcome. This is where the government can play a positive role in facilitating and catalysing a change in business climate. Governments do not have to legislate and regulate to effect change. They can exercise their authority and unique skills to facilitate corporate social responsibility. This is best achieved when governments and business endeavour to use the power of partnership to their advantage, with the state playing a facilitation role in bringing communities, interest groups, businesses and environmental concerns together. This should be based on voluntary action by businesses and civil society; the role of the government is in creating opportunities for these partnerships to develop and in supporting them with flexible policies and regulations.

An excellent example of facilitation is the Nordic Swan, an eco-label established by the Nordic Council of Ministers in 1989.[62] This is a voluntary organisation established to facilitate eco-labelling of environmentally sound products and services. Focused on three main product types — daily care, building and energy, and business-to-business — the Nordic Swan is a recognised leader in environmental assurance within Europe. This is based on quality standards, which are reviewed every three years to constantly improve environmental performance along the 'criteria escalator'. These standards — precisely because they are worked out through consultation with state authorities, industry groups, consumers and environmental organisations — have high rates of compliance and continue to lead the world in defining environmental quality criteria. Notably the Nordic Swan has achieved this by taking a pro-business attitude:

> We tell all the companies, we are here to provide a tool — for you to use your environmental aspect as a tool of competition. We are here to give you [businesses] an opportunity to make money because you are good on environmental aspects. We tell consumers that the best company should get the best money.[63]

By facilitating companies' strategic CSR policies, Nordic Swan is now at a stage where it is run as a business, with only 10% of its funding coming from the government. The remainder of funding comes from company contributions. The fact that over 1,000 businesses belong to Nordic Swan within Sweden shows that businesses believe there to be a benefit in membership. If there was no shared value creation then Nordic Swan could not exist. But as a labelling agency it has to have strict standards to maintain its value and legitimacy, balancing between business and public interests. This is where the active involvement of environmental groups, civil society and communities in the consultation process for new standards is necessary. Because of the broad base of business, public and government support, the Nordic Swan is a good example of flexible policy instruments at work.

This is one example of the role that governments can play in facilitating and enabling, rather than legislating and regulating, to encourage responsible corporate behaviour. As with any partnership, it draws together the key strengths, the core competences, of each partner and leverages these to maximum effect. Opportunities exist for governments to help businesses address their CSR in a number of ways: by consulting with them on social and environmental legislation, by encouraging communities to consult with businesses directly and by supporting industry best practice. But, as with any policy instrument, facilitation is the right tool for only some jobs; for other instances regulations are required and it is crucial that this is done responsibly.

Regulating responsibility

Taking into account the need for flexible regulation, governments must still be very cautious about regulating corporate social responsibility. Any attempts to define exactly what form of responsibility companies should engage in removes the competitive nature of strategic CSR. Companies need to compete, to innovate and create new opportunities for CSR. Legislating how companies should do this risks reducing competition and creating less public good. This threatens to make CSR a cost, instead of an opportunity for strategic advantage. As the Business Council of Australia pointed out:

> Mandating CSR through legislative intervention runs the risk of sti-
> fling the innovation and creative approaches to CSR that are being
> adopted by Australian companies . . . The greatest social contribu-
> tion made by corporations is through employment, the goods and
> services they create and the wealth these produce (BCA Submission
> to Parliamentary Committee).[64]

Happily, the parliamentary committee in Australia decided against compulsion, recognising that CSR should be encouraged (not mandated) using partnerships and government-led initiatives. This does not rule out regulation: for example, the Australian Corporations Act (2001) requires companies with 'particular and significant' environmental impacts to report these annually as part of their directors' statements (Blake, Dawson, Waldron Lawyers 2006), but this allows companies to tailor strategic CSR policies to suit their specific business strategy. Moreover, flexible enforcement of environmental regulations allows companies to innovate and gain competitive advantage from protecting the environment in novel ways.

In Kazakhstan, my clients face a very different approach. Government pressure on companies to subsidise local schools and hospitals has been driven by requests from local mayors and elites, with companies now seeing 'CSR' as just another form of tax. This has meant that money has been spent on projects of no shared commercial and community benefit. Companies are contributing cash but not expertise, failing to leverage their core competences and in some cases contributing to corruption. Sadly, this spending buys neither regional development nor local legitimacy. To quote one mining executive: 'Kazakhstan doesn't need any more felt workshops or *dombra*[65] classes; it needs rural regional infrastructure and local access to jobs.'

What this points out is the fine line between the state regulating to suit its interests (which remain crucial) and CSR contributing to local needs. Inevitably, there is a need for a balance: companies must negotiate between meeting the needs and demands of all their stakeholders (investors, host governments, employees, local communities) and aiming to create shared value for their shareholders and society. But, when governments seek to legislate and regulate specific forms of CSR, it is dangerous indeed.

What governments can do, however, is set rules that encourage and enable responsible investment. This can include providing tax incentives for long-term social investment, in much the same way as corporate research and development receives tax relief. Likewise, by working with industry to set minimum standards and voluntary schemes for leading firms, governments can act as enablers of social investment. This will require the government to act as a partner in developing and expanding best practices, playing a role as a knowledge broker and enabler, rather than strictly a regulator. There will always be a role for establishing legal minimum standards, but a flexible approach that provides the right *incentives* for responsibility is the greatest contribution the government can make to the new business climate.

Incentives for responsibility

As we have seen with voluntary carbon trading schemes, companies will innovate and develop strategies to reduce business costs when a sound business case exists to do so. What is essential is that the costs and benefits, to society and the company, are fully accounted for. Historically, adverse social and environmental costs have been 'externalised' by companies. These costs have thus fallen on poor countries and poor communities, while the profit has been sequestered towards the rich world and the private sector. That this is resented, in anti-globalisation protests and boycotts, is unsurprising. In order to bring about a change in business climate, governments need to create the correct incentives for companies to act responsibly. This is not an anti-business approach. On the contrary, new business opportunities, new possibilities for profit, can be created when governments set the right incentives for responsible innovation.

By creating policies that ensure companies fully account for the impact of their actions, the power of the marketplace can be used to create public good. If both rich and poor governments collaborate, with civil society and businesses, to measure the 'true' environmental and social impact, then companies will be pursuing their own, and public, interests in taking measures to reduce these costs. It is through this mechanism that companies will use their core competences (business development, supply chain management, financial acumen) in partnership with the public and NGO sector, to promote poverty alleviation and environmental protection. The challenge is in getting this to work. I identify here three *opportunities* for responsible regulation by governments: environmental pricing, social investment incentives and labelling initiatives.

Environmental pricing

Some environmentalists would claim that the environment is priceless, that no amount of money can buy or replace the environment. To an extent, for unique habitats and endangered species, they are perhaps right. But the fact is that, in everyday activities, we are constantly making choices that have an impact on the environment. Given that most economic decisions, buying and selling, are made on the question of price, it seems logical to include the 'price' of environmental degradation in the cost of an item. By getting the 'pricing right' governments can then leave it to businesses to compete and innovate to lower their costs, and in so doing, reduce their environmental impact.

Putting a price on the environment is not easy, 'not least because the benefits frequently do not have a market value and are not tangible — how can you measure the value of a beautiful view, or a less noisy street?' (OECD 2007). But it is possible to determine proxy figures for the value of environmental damage, using economic tools such as quantifying consumer stated and revealed preferences, and calculating use and non-use value. Another method is to determine the 'clean-up' cost for the pollution, such as planting forests as 'carbon sinks' to offset CO_2 emissions from industry. This 'value' of the environment can then determine pollution pricing, using the market pricing instruments of supply and demand.

Transport is one industry in which this pollution pricing is long overdue. For historical reasons jet fuel is not taxed, so there is the equivalent of a subsidy for air transport over other (perhaps more eco-friendly) forms of transport, such as road or rail. This is an issue that has gained a lot of attention recently, especially because of the link between CO_2 emissions and climate change. BA's voluntary carbon offset programme is a useful start, but environmental pricing has to be uniform across an industry to allow the market to function properly. Currently consumers are making choices, such as deciding not to buy Kenyan cut flowers and fresh vegetables, which are flown to the UK daily, on the basis of an environmental choice. But, because of the complexity of global supply chains, this may not be helping the environment at all.

Because of the cold European winter, sometimes energy use is higher for domestically grown crops than for imported ones. New Zealand lamb, although it is sent from 12 time zones away, is still more energy-efficient than British lamb sold on the London high street (*The Economist* 2006). The recent consumer swing against air-delivered produce is also causing a lot of hardship in poor rural communities that have invested in producing export products (Averill 2007). The only way to make purchasing decisions transparent, and to encourage genuine innovation and energy reduction within an industry, is by applying an economic cost to this pollution and taxing it accordingly. Environmental pricing helps businesses and consumers understand their environmental impact accurately. Only governments can enforce such initiatives, which is why governments need to take the lead in creating the right economic incentives for environmental responsibility.

Social investment incentives

When companies invest in R&D spending, they usually benefit from a tax rebate. This recognises that R&D spending is an investment in creating future returns for the company, and that some of these benefits will 'spill over' into society. Likewise, in many jurisdictions, contributions to charities can be written off against tax liabilities, creating a 'cheap' form of PR for businesses and helping to support NGOs. Individual giving to charity is encouraged through similar tax rebates on income tax. What does not exist in most jurisdictions is a tax rebate or other financial incentive to explicitly encourage corporate social responsibility.

There would be real benefits in applying the lessons of R&D tax incentives to CSR investment. Companies would need to prove that their CSR spending is an investment in creating shared value both for the company and for society, not just charitable giving. This acknowledgment by governments of the long-term nature of strategic CSR investment would encourage what is already occurring in the financial markets: a recognition that CSR is an investment in long-term corporate and social prosperity. It is an investment in creating shared value. By creating accounting and tax incentives for social investment, governments are playing their role in encouraging companies to align profit motive with the public good.

This would also help companies to weather the criticism that sometimes comes from investors, that by spending on CSR they are 'destroying shareholder value'. Some companies, especially those taking the 'cookie-cutter' or 'charity' approach to CSR, do destroy shareholder value. But those companies that stick to their core competence, partner, localise and innovate, are investing in shared value creation. It is appropriate that governments begin to recognise this, by providing tax and accounting incentives for social investment.

Labelling initiatives and standards

Eco-labels, fair-trade certifications and environmental packaging have proliferated in recent years. For the uninitiated consumer, these can confuse more than inform, and there is a growing level of cynicism that companies, especially high-street supermarkets, are using labelling as a way to increase their profit margins from discretionary consumers. Fair-trade labelling organisations have done an excellent job in getting issues of child labour, unfair trade, environmental damage and uneven trade subsidies onto the political agenda and into the public consciousness. But labelled goods, in all their forms, still only make up a small part of the total market and are generally restricted to consumer-oriented products.

This is where governments can play a facilitation role in promoting clear and understandable eco-labels. The Nordic Swan example is one instance of how a specific approach has worked well in one part of the world. However, in different regions where citizens have a different perspective of their governments, a modified model will be required. The novel contribution that governments can make, unlike labelling organisations, is that they are easily identifiable and accountable. By setting state standards, voluntary or compulsory, governments can help companies gain competitive advantage through their corporate social responsibility programmes. This is part of a gradual step towards flexible regulations, which allows the state to build partnerships with businesses and provides an opportunity for companies to evolve their supply chains.

Stopping free-riders

One of the biggest challenges that responsible companies face is the problem of free-riders. If companies take initiatives to lead the field, say in refusing to pay bribes or in protecting the environment, they risk being undercut by less responsible corporations. When companies are going beyond legal minimums, especially working in the hard industries in the developing world, they can be beaten by a competitor in a 'race to the bottom'. It is a source of frustration to company leaders that they take a responsible decision, say, on how to conduct their joint venture for oil exploration in a developing country, which means their bid cost is

Box 5 **Thought provoker: from slave trade to fair trade?**

Two hundred years ago, on 25 March 1807, slavery was outlawed in the British Empire. The success of legislation outlawing slavery was based on a campaign that pioneered many of the tactics in use today by the fair-trade lobby. Boycotts, information campaigns, labelling, public protests and petitions were all used to force slave traders out of business and to encourage the government to take action. These same tactics are used today in the fight against child labour, unfair trade and environmental damage, and they have been effective in putting the issue of fair trade on the political and business agenda.

Creating awareness of the problem of slavery was crucial to the success of the protests: civil-society organisations spread the word through newspapers, pamphlets and public speeches. But, in an age of illiteracy, the most enduring image of the abolition campaign was that of the slave ship *Brookes*. This was a cross-section, presented to the Privy Council in 1788, showing the awful conditions onboard a slave ship (Hochschild 2005). It pictured how 482 slaves were stowed as cargo in the ship, laid side by side, with children filling in the gaps in the rounding of the bow.

In 1791, pamphlets were printed that encouraged people to boycott sugar from the West Indies which was produced with slave labour. The boycott was joined by 300,000 people, with sales dropping by up to 50%. Businesses responded, just as they do today, by innovating. For example the East India Company marketed its sugar as 'not made by Slaves', increasing its sales tenfold over two years. This was during a time when sugar was big business; Britain had even considered keeping the sugar island of Guadeloupe in exchange for returning Canada to the French, at the Peace of Paris in 1763. Because of its importance, it was only an act of parliament that could end, rather than reduce, the slave trade. Finally, public pressure grew to such an extent that in 1807 slavery was outlawed.

Once British businesses could no longer be involved in the slave trade, it was in their interests to make sure their competitors could not either. Acting both from moral righteousness and financial self-interest, British businesses encouraged the government to enforce the slavery ban on the high seas. As the nautical power of the time, the British navy resolutely enforced the slavery ban on foreign competitors, preventing them from gaining an economic advantage from British

continued opposite →

abolition. This helped prevent the 'free-rider' problem, of slave-trading nations profiting from British abolition.

It would seem that, having copied so many of the tactics and campaign tools of the abolitionists, the next move for the fair-trade lobby would be to push to make fair labour standards (such as banning child labour) mandatory. If the economic powers of today, Europe, America and the large multinational companies, do decide to outlaw unfair labour and trade, they have the means to enforce it globally. Once fair labour standards become the norm, it is in the financial interests of compliant companies and countries to make sure their competitors also comply. The challenge for the responsible corporation is to decide whether they want to lead, or simply follow, the development of these global labour standards and the growth of public support for fair trade.

higher and that they do not pay bribes to gain the contract. If these responsible companies are constantly undercut by irresponsible companies, which will often also lack the worker rights and environmental concerns that a responsible corporation brings, then this is unsustainable. Governments have a role to play here in preventing 'free-riders' from gaining an advantage. This can only be achieved by making and enforcing legal minimum standards that reward, rather than punish, responsible corporations. This raises the playing field, but it keeps the playing field level for all operators, encouraging competition. Such an approach is part of bringing about a new business climate that encourages sustainability and responsible corporate behaviour.

An interesting example of how government action, in concert with corporations and with public consultation, has led to improved social and environmental performance can be found in Norway. By taking a deliberately 'market-based' approach, tailored to suit the needs of the country, the Norwegian government has helped to reduce electrical waste (thus creating social and environmental value) without damaging investor value. Indeed, new business opportunities have arisen from this pro-business *and* pro-environment policy.

Case study: electrical waste policy in Norway

A good example of flexible government policy is Norway's regulation on electrical and electronic (EE) waste. This policy reduces costs, raises compliance and drives innovation. The Norwegian government's approach engaged producers, importers and distributors from the outset. The concept behind the policy is that EE waste is damaging for the environment and that the best way to reduce the amount of harmful waste is through extended producer responsibility (EPR). This market-oriented approach tries to 'get the prices right' by ensuring that those companies that produce polluting waste are responsible for its clean-up. This encourages innovation, with economic incentives for companies to reduce their ecological footprint. What it does not do, however, is impose inflexible rules on industry which would increase business costs and discourage innovation. Instead, it works at creating a business climate in which governments and companies work in partnership towards waste reduction.

To implement the policy the environmental authorities, major firms and business associations developed agreement for the 'take-back' of EE waste. The Norwegian Pollution Control Authority (SFT) created a partnership with industry that relied on trust and shared value creation. The policy is worth examining in some detail, to help understand how it came about, how it functions today and the benefits that each party gains from this flexible policy. What we see is that governments, by changing the business climate, can create partnerships that drive innovation and economic growth, while protecting the environment and creating public good.

Background to the policy

In 1999, Norway was among the first countries in the world to implement a policy of EPR for waste electrical and electronic (EE) goods (Lee and Røine 2004). The approach, encouraging industry to take responsibility for their waste through a 'take-back' system, was novel. But the unique origins of the policy date back several years to a covenant agreement, signed between industry and the government, that can be seen as 'soft regulation'. This gave businesses a chance to adapt their activities to meet government waste reduction goals without excessive cost.

This covenant, worked out from 1995 to 1998, was essential in building trust between the government and industry. Recognising that the policy would only be successful if the regulations were developed cooperatively, the government established 'working groups' of industry bodies to find common solutions to the shared responsibility of EE waste. The decision to adopt a voluntary 'take-back' programme was only possible because these working groups established a business climate of mutual understanding: 'The system depends a lot on trust. We built up a system based on trust – it is easier for both parties to then see the benefit of the regulation.'[66]

Inherent in this approach is a realistic approach to environmental regulation. The Norwegian government recognised that businesses, if given the right incentives, would become environmentally responsible – but that this responsibility had to be grounded in creating profit. Likewise, industry groups recognised that they could choose between inflexible regulations, with a high cost, and engaging in the process and attempting to reduce costs, increase compliance and seek future opportunities. By creating 'working groups' the government and industry were able to communicate with each other, sharing their ideas on how to confront the problem of EE waste and arriving at common solutions. This *consensual* approach to regulation meant that the EE policy presented a low cost for businesses and ensured high rates of waste 'take-back' for the government. To quote one SFT staff member summarising the policy: 'We trusted the market and the market worked.'[67]

This is not to leave environmental protection just to the market. Rather, it recognises that the market itself will very often not take care of the environment, so regulation is needed. Thus the incentives must be so strong and effective that compliance becomes the most *profitable* way forward. The 'trust' in market forces uses regulation to harness, instead of fighting, the market forces.

How it works in practice

Consumers can leave their EE waste, free of charge, at drop-off points established by municipalities and at any retail outlet. There are 2,500 active drop-off points in Norway, and consumers can drop off their waste at any depot, even if the item was initially purchased from a different location. This 'collective' responsibility was actually favoured by industry groups over individual responsibility, on the basis that it was more practical and cost-effective. Interestingly, the EU initially considered adopting individual responsibility (i.e. only goods purchased from a particular supplier could be returned to that same supplier) as it was more market-oriented and incentive-based. But consultation for the EU directive identified that industry preferred collective responsibility, resulting in lower costs and higher collection rates. Norway adopted collective responsibility from the outset because of its practicality.

To deal with EE waste, three new producer responsibility organisations were formed, on industry initiative, which take responsibility for waste collection, processing and recycling. These companies, Elektronikkretur and Hvitevareretur (now merged into El-retur), covering most of the consumer EE waste, and Renas, mostly covering EE waste from professional users, are run on a not-for-profit basis. Together these take-back companies cover all kinds of EE waste, sharing product groups between them. Funding is provided by domestic producers and importers on a sliding scale; in the El-retur system producers pay a fixed fee for the products they sell — for instance, US$10 for a household washing machine and US$1 for a telephone — but it is important to note that these costs are determined by the 'market', without regulatory interference.

> This, to some extent, obeys the 'polluter pays principle'. However, while this simple fee structure may help to achieve higher administrative efficiency, it does not seem to provide incentives for producers to make their products environmentally superior . . . *there is no clear mechanism to stimulate green products* (Lee and Røine 2004).

What this means is that there are no specific incentives for producers to reduce the levels of EE in their products, as the polluting pricing does not reflect the amount of waste produced. At first sight this seems to be a policy shortcoming, but what closer analysis reveals is that it is rather a good example of realistic, not idealistic, policy-making. Because Norway imports over 90% of its electronic goods, the ability to influence foreign manufacturers is in reality limited. But, for those EE industries in which Norway is strong, for instance in cable production, it is possible for individual producers to 'opt out' of the common system and establish their own 'take-back' programmes. This policy flexibility allows for industries to innovate and compete, while setting the incentives to ensure that this competition leads to greater, rather than less, policy enforcement. It is not a perfect system, and recent changes have been necessary to reduce the free-rider problem, but as a policy it has been very effective at reducing EE waste without placing undue costs on producers and consumers.

Who benefits?

Norway's EE waste policy can be deemed a 'win–win–win' strategy. The natural environment benefits from a reduction in the amount of EE waste and hazardous substances. The government benefits from implementing a policy, which creates public good, without placing high administrative or enforcement costs on the pollution control agency or other state body. Likewise, business also benefits — both from having a low-cost, predictable and flexible form of regulation, and through new business opportunities coming about from the changed business climate for EE waste.

EE and the environment

Electrical and electronic waste has a large environmental impact. Although EE waste constitutes only about 5% of total household waste, EE goods typically include hazardous materials such as lead, flame retardants, cadmium and mercury. The ecological impact of these substances, if improperly treated, is considerable: polluting waterways, impacting on fisheries and risking human well-being. Thus any reduction in (a) the amount of EE waste entering the environment, and (b) the quantities of hazardous waste in EE goods, constitutes a positive development for the environment. The results to date have been impressive. In 2006, 68,277 tonnes (14.7 kg per capita) of EE waste was collected for environmentally sound recycling, from which over 6,000 tonnes of hazardous substances were separated for safe disposal.[68] If we compare this with the EU target of 4 kg per capita, we see from Figure 13 that Norway is well ahead. The positive impact that this has on the natural environment is considerable and, as importantly, the policy lays the future framework for continued innovation and improvement, in a way that inflexible regulation would fail to do.

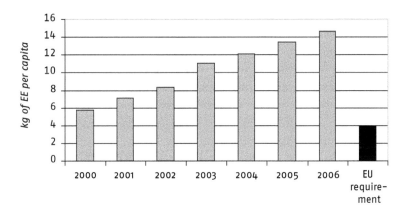

Figure 13 **Norway's EE waste returned per capita**

Source: Data courtesy of El-retur, www.elretur.no (accessed 8 May 2008)

Government benefit

In creating the EE waste policy, the Norwegian Ministry of the Environment and the Pollution Control Authority set the target of collecting 80% of EE waste by 2004. In reality this 80% goal was achieved by 2003, and by 2004 over 90% of EE waste was collected. This policy target has been achieved without the necessity of creating expensive enforcement mechanisms and, while from 1 July 2007 all 'take-back' companies need SFT approval, the administrative costs to the government remain small. What the Norwegian government has also witnessed is an increasing industry emphasis on the *recycling* of existing waste and *prevention* of hazardous waste. Because of the awareness-raising aspect of the EE policy, and because industry bodies were engaged in the working groups, the awareness of hazardous waste issues has risen among businesses. This has led to waste reduction strategies from businesses, beyond what was envisaged or targeted in the original EE policy. Once involved in this programme, companies then have an interest to ensure that their competitors also comply, which ensures higher levels of compliance than in a state regulation system. Perhaps as important for future work, SFT staff discuss how their trust relationships with industry enable them to respond quickly to new environmental challenges, which is important for constantly updating flexible policy instruments.

Commercial benefit

Perhaps most surprising for an environmental regulation, businesses have also seen a commercial benefit. While the administration of the 'take-back' schemes is an undeniable cost, this is much lower than it could otherwise be. Because a collective responsibility system was adopted, using private-sector capabilities for the producer responsibility organisations, the cost to industry has been approximately 0.1% of the retail price for most goods. This sort of cost increase can be absorbed by the producer and, to an extent, passed on to the consumer. Businesses involved in the process have been able to reduce the cost of regulation by being engaged early on, in the 'covenant' on EE waste and in supporting the 'take-back' producer responsibility organisations.

As noted, Norway is not a major producer or exporter of EE goods, so the downstream impacts on other markets are limited. However, because Norway has adopted an EE policy early on, some firms are now beginning to use their expertise at waste reduction in foreign markets where EE regulations are now being introduced. This 'first to market' commercial advantage is discussed in detail below. But perhaps the greatest advantage for companies is that they can continue to do business in Norway, with long-term certainty on what the regulations will be, and companies can make long-term investment decisions based on predictable and responsive regulation.

Flexible policy driving innovation

Norway, by taking a lead on EE waste management, has created commercial opportunities for companies. It has also facilitated the process of technological innovation in both downstream and upstream industries, leading to reduced EE waste and helping Norwegian companies to benefit from the 'first to market' advantage.

Downstream and upstream innovation

Downstream businesses, those distributing and retailing electrical goods in Norway, have made a number of important process innovations as a result of the EE regulation. This includes the creation of dedicated 'take-back' services that change the supply chain and end-of-life recovery chain of EE waste. Several evolutionary innovations have occurred to make this possible, including the development of new techniques for recycling and recovery in a high-labour-cost country. Perhaps most revolutionary has been the development of new technologies to deal with hazardous waste, including the world's first SF6 treatment plant (Lee and Røine 2004). This man-made gas, used in electrical switching equipment, is a major risk for global warming (1 tonne of SF6 is equivalent to 25,000 tonnes of CO_2). It was only with the introduction of the EE regulations that the incentives, and awareness, existed to encourage the development of SF6 disposal technology. Now that these innovations have been made to work in Norway, as a lead market, opportunities exist for businesses to export these new process innovations to new markets, especially within the EU.

Upstream innovation, in the production of EE goods is made more difficult by Norway's status as an importer of EE goods. As a small country, Norway's ability to influence global production is limited. However, because the EU's Waste Electric and Electronic Equipment Directive (WEEE) (2003) adopted much of Norway's policy, there is certainly a wider impact. Likewise, initiatives that start in Norway often 'spill over' into other markets. For instance, Osram, one of the world's leading lighting manufacturers, decided in 2003 to begin production of lead-free incandescent lamps. This product innovation meant the removal of lead in both the glass and the solder of new lamps produced in Norway. While not compulsory, Osram chose to show leadership on this issue, recognising their corporate responsibility to do so, reflecting also how the use of flexible regulation has 'spill-over' effects on corporate behaviour.

First to market: EU WEEE and Tomra

One of the biggest commercial benefits that can come from early policy adoption is the 'first to market' advantage. This is where companies, working in leading markets, gain expertise and experience that allows them to compete in other markets more effectively.[69] For example companies that have management systems in place to manage their environmental impacts can leverage these systems into new markets, where existing competitors lack these skills. As the EE regulations in Norway are a recently introduced policy, there are as yet few examples of how being 'first to market' has helped companies. However, in cases such as the SF6 treatment plant, the potential is obvious. Also, as the EU adopts the WEEE Directive, opportunities for Norwegian companies to leverage their expertise will emerge. This is certainly the case with an older example of EPR: the return of recyclable bottles. Again, Norway was a leader in this policy and Tomra, a company making automated bottle collection machines, has been able to leverage this early experience to become the leader in this rapidly growing global market.

Conclusions

Governments set the business climate in which companies operate. As this chapter shows, if companies are to act responsibly, to take advantage of the *opportunities* of corporate social responsibility, then we need a new business climate, moving towards a regulatory and legal environment that rewards responsible corporate behaviour. This can be achieved in a way that delivers value to responsible corporations, creating incentives for companies to create value for society. By aligning more directly public good with private profit, governments can help deliver shared value.

This change in business climate is about recognising that governments, businesses and civil society each contribute in different ways to a healthy society and economy. To achieve the best outcomes, governments are best advised to seek to work with – not against – businesses. Seeking collaboration and cooperation is a way to create shared value, both for business and for society. Good regulation and the rule of law are still essential; there should be no collusion between the state and business interests. But in seeking to address social and environmental issues, governments and businesses have a shared responsibility. This can be achieved by setting the 'rules of the game', such as creating incentives for social investment, introducing environmental pricing and implementing flexible, responsive regulations. In this way governments can facilitate society, and encourage businesses, to find shared solutions to common problems. By taking a cooperative approach governments can create an enabling environment for CSR. Governments must remain separate from businesses, but by getting the 'rules of the game' right and by contributing the unique competences that only governments can offer, there is potential for shared value creation.

7
Non-governmental organisations

Non-governmental organisations (NGOs) are an inevitable part of CSR. Wherever in the world your business operates, in whatever industry and however you aim to implement your CSR strategy, NGOs are a usual part of the mix. As partners they can be excellent, awful or somewhere in-between. NGOs can ensure the success of your CSR strategy or they can call its very viability into question. NGOs have real power, which is not always used in the most *responsible* manner. Ensuring that your company's engagement with NGOs is positive requires an understanding of who and what NGOs are, how they operate and how you should – and should not – attempt to engage with NGOs. If properly managed, NGO collaboration can form a crucial part of your CSR strategy. NGOs can contribute a great deal and their capacities and skills complement those of the private sector.

Understanding how NGOs operate is crucial. NGOs are not like businesses, although many of them (contrary to what you might think) do turn a tidy profit. NGOs are not necessarily charities, although some are – doing excellent work in difficult parts of the world. In fact actually pinning down who and what constitutes an NGO is a bit of a challenge, as I will explain in this chapter. This is why you need to focus on *defining* what sort of NGO partner you want to work with and *identifying a strategy* to engage with the right sort of NGO. As with any business partner, you need to understand how NGOs operate. In this chapter we look at the 'business model' for NGOs. Understanding the way in which NGOs raise their money in business terms of 'making sales' helps to understand why NGOs — often presenting themselves as bastions of charity — have their own interests, and why it is important to understand these interests, in order to build successful collaborations. By understanding the business model of NGOs, it is possible to head off potential future problems and adverse publicity, as part of a CSR strategy.

Crucial to understanding NGOs is the issue of accountability. NGOs have grown immensely in profile and power in recent years, yet this growing influence, amid calls for businesses to be more accountable and open, has not always led to greater accountability and responsibility in the NGO sector. Addressing this 'democratic deficit' requires improved governance within the NGO sector. The responsibility for this lies with the NGO sector itself, but companies can avoid problems by choosing carefully which NGOs they partner with and how.

The message of this chapter is clear: NGO partnerships, if properly managed, can be very productive. NGOs have a wide range of capacities, legitimacy and local contacts that companies don't have — and would struggle to develop themselves. But NGOs are not perfect — there are some real problems with how their business model operates and the lack of accountability in the sector. This is why a well-formulated CSR programme will include a strategy for working with NGOs, along with other partners. Doing this requires an understanding of what NGOs are, how their business model operates, the strengths and weaknesses of the sector, and how to engage with NGO partners effectively.

Who and what are NGOs?

'Non-governmental organisations' is a very broad term, encompassing a wide diversity of groups. NGOs range from the very small to the very big, from the local to the global, from constructive to obstructive, from excellent partners to liabilities. These NGOs are all part of 'civil society', the innocuous group that is not governmental and is not for profit. Alongside defining what NGOs are 'not', it is sometimes a little unclear what exactly NGOs 'are'. In a much-used definition, the World Bank defines NGOs as:

> Private organizations that pursue activities to relieve suffering, promote the interests of the poor, protect the environment, provide basic social services, or undertake community development. NGOs often differ from other organizations in the sense that they tend to operate independent from government, are value-based and are generally guided by principles of community and cooperation.[70]

This is a wide definition. It could potentially include private companies with a strong social mandate, such as private organisations that promote employment and economic development which in turn 'relieve suffering' and 'provide social services'. But few would include companies in this list; NGOs are 'not for profit' (although the more successful produce 'surpluses') so companies are excluded from being NGOs. However, these lines are blurred, especially with the growth of NGOs that provide consultancy and implementation services to donor agencies — NGOs which in essence exist to provide employment for the founders. You are not alone if you think that this all sounds rather confusing, that it looks like a lot of definitions based on what organisations are 'not'. Defining an NGO is difficult. To paraphrase Churchill (when trying to define trade unions):

> Although it can be very difficult to define what is or what is not an NGO — most people know an NGO when they see one. It is like trying to define a rhinoceros; it is difficult enough, but if one is seen, everybody can recognise it.

This is why we need to understand a bit more about the different forms of NGOs that work around the world and begin to understand how the subtlety of different NGOs can influence how you choose to build partnerships. In general there are two types of NGO:

- **Operational NGOs** who see their role in the planning and implementation of development projects. These operational NGOs can be very locally focused, national or international

- **Advocacy NGOs** whose function is to defend or promote a specific cause or issue. Advocacy NGOs often seek to influence the policies and practices of companies through tactics such as 'name and shame' and adverse publicity

These two categories are not mutually exclusive. A growing number of NGOs, especially international NGOs, engage in both operational and advocacy activities — many advocacy NGOs that work in the developed world will implement projects through local operational partners in the developing world, using an outsourcing model. Some advocacy NGOs, while not directly involved in designing and implementing projects, will fund specific projects that are related to their advocacy campaigns, thus showing that they are 'making a difference'. In forming partnerships with NGOs the clearest opportunity for cooperation is operational collaboration, building partnerships to implement projects. This is not to rule out policy dialogue with advocacy NGOs, which also holds considerable potential, especially in preventing adverse publicity.

Operational NGOs

Operational NGOs run projects; they seek funding for specific or general activities and then implement their projects, either directly or through partner organisations. The operations that each organisation undertakes are a reflection of their comparative size, scope, aims and capacities. This can include community-based organisations (CBOs), which are grass-roots membership organisations with clearly defined geographic focus and often a focus on a specific issue or group: for example, a women's group in a rural area, which focuses on self-help initiatives which are largely self-financed, or have a stable supply of external funding.

National or regional organisations often have a mix of operational and advocacy roles; the operations are based on receiving *and* disbursing money. Fundraising focuses on domestic and international sources, often supplementing donations with paid work for aid agencies, direct funding requests for projects to donor governments and philanthropic organisations. Operations are often monitored and supported with technical input from national NGOs, with actual implementation taking place through CBOs or local affiliates/offices of the national NGO. In the same manner, international NGOs coordinate sector-wide projects (i.e. focused on a specific issue or area) across multiple countries. Their skill is in raising funding for large projects from corporate and private donations and public-sector donors (e.g. the World Bank, national governments), then bringing international best practices into different countries to make these projects work.

Advocacy NGOs

Advocacy NGOs take a different approach; they focus not on implementing change themselves but on building awareness and public understanding of issues in an attempt to effect greater change. Often this has taken the form of attacks on companies or entire industries, hoping to gain funding for operational NGOs (or partners) and trying to promote policy or legal changes. Sometimes these advocacy NGOs can be useful partners in identifying issues, but there is constant friction arising from the fact that advocacy NGOs gain their publicity and funding through headlines and 'shocking' stories. There are few guarantees that these stories are always fair and, once attacked, companies can find it very difficult to present their side of the story. The public perception, played out in the media, of companies as inherently 'bad' and NGOs as inherently 'good' and reliable, is still strong, so there is certainly cause for caution in dealing with advocacy NGOs. That said, a proactive approach is best in heading off potential problems.

Because of the number and diversity of operational NGOs it is dangerous to make generalisations about how different projects are implemented. Some CBOs are excellent and have genuine grass-roots contacts and skills. Others are little more than a cover for the local elite to reinforce their status, subsidised with donor money. As with businesses, or any other group, it is unfair to characterise NGOs as inherently good or bad; the reality is much more complex. Which is why you need to understand which NGOs you are working with and how they conduct their operational and advocacy roles, or how their 'business model' works.

The NGO business model

NGOs, like any other organisation, rely on money to operate. Whether they are operational- or advocacy-focused, NGOs need to raise funding to conduct their operations and fulfil their aims. There is nothing wrong with this, but it is important to understand how this affects the way NGOs function and the sorts of partnership that NGOs seek. NGO fundraising is *problem*-oriented; that is to say, NGOs raise funding by identifying *problems* which they then claim to be able to *resolve*, given the right resources. The problem can range from immediate issues, such as a famine in a certain area or the response to a natural disaster, or more long-term issues such as childhood nutrition and malaria prevention. The greater the problem, the greater the ability of the NGO to make a publicity impact and gain more funding for its solution (advocacy, operations or a mix of both). This is where *new* problems have greater sales potential; they are more likely to gain publicity and to win funding. So there is a pressure to identify and develop new problems to renew donor sympathy and gain funding.

Succeeding as an NGO requires money, which requires a solid business model. The basis of this business model consists of four steps, which form a cycle. These steps are: issue identification, investigation and publicity, fundraising and, finally, action. This cycle is detailed in Figure 14.

Identifying issues or problems is the first step for NGOs. Most focus on a specific problem or sector. UNICEF focuses on children, Oxfam works on advocacy around the issue of poverty, whereas local NGOs will often confront more locally specific issues. Many of the well-known NGOs have established issues on which they work, whereas newcomers must come up with new problems or an innovative approach to solving these problems. As with any industry, being the first to identify a new issue (or, cynically, opportunity), such as organic coffee or fairtrade clothes, presents the 'first to market' benefit. The bigger, more sensational, unusual or devastating the problem the greater the likelihood of the second step

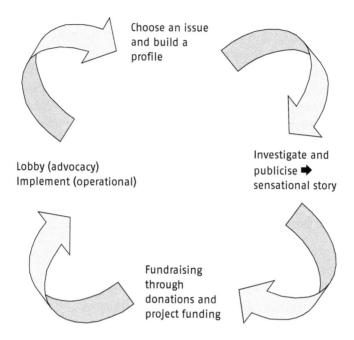

Choose an issue and build a profile

Investigate and publicise ➡ sensational story

Lobby (advocacy) Implement (operational)

Fundraising through donations and project funding

Figure 14 **NGO business model**

working. Likewise, coming up with new implementation ideas, such as 'retail giving' where consumers buy a gift card that funds, for example, a goat in southern Sudan, helps to build the profile of the NGO. Success in choosing an issue that gains public attention lays the groundwork for the next stage.

This second step is to 'investigate' or publicise an issue: to put a problem on the public agenda and in the media cycle. For an issue that is already at the forefront of public attention, such as the Asian tsunami, NGOs seek to establish themselves as *the* organisation that can help solve the problem. Media campaigns during these events tend to emphasise the length of time the NGO has been working in the region and how its specific expertise allows it to help; if you like, it emphasises its comparative advantage over other NGOs. With 'new' issues, publicity tends to take the form of an 'education' campaign, to create public awareness. This is typically based on, often very partial, investigation or 'research' conducted by the NGO. These reports focus on finding sensational or headline-grabbing facts and are often given suggestive or emotive titles that claim to expose the 'truth'. Examples include 'The True Price of Diamonds'[71] and 'White Gold: The True Cost of Cotton – Uzbekistan, Cotton and the Crushing of a Nation' (Environmental Justice Foundation 2005). The focus here is not on solving the problem, or even on necessarily presenting a full picture, but on building up enough public indignation and sympathy that people, or organisations, open their wallets. This leads to the third step in the cycle.

Ultimately, NGOs need money to pay staff salaries, to cover operational costs, to recover the expense of research and publicity and to fund advocacy campaigns or operations. Much of this is important work, relying on voluntary contributions and dedicated staff; it is not to be belittled. But it is also not to be misunderstood. Increasingly, the NGO sector is a competitive industry, with multiple actors competing for scarce funds. Professional fundraisers now feature prominently in all major NGOs and the role of founders and managers in smaller organisations is often largely one of raising funds and winning project funding.

This money is then spent on implementation and advocacy, as well as being 'reinvested' in future research and publicity. As a rough guide, 5–8% of all donations will be absorbed in the head office of an international NGO, as part of the cost of fundraising. The actual implementation of projects ranges from the excellent to the incompetent, from the life-changing to the irredeemably corrupt. It is dangerous to generalise. The crucial thing to recognise from a risk management perspective is that your company will increasingly be held liable for the impacts of donations. Shareholders expect a decent return on investments in CSR, and other NGOs in this competitive industry are quick to criticise ineffectual projects from other providers. Giving money is not enough; you need to monitor how this money is spent and be actively engaged in the projects, contributing expertise, core competences and staff time.

Once the project is implemented, NGOs then need to find continued funding for ongoing activities and new sources of finance for new initiatives. The constant cycle starts again: raising money by creating publicity, conducting 'research' and building public awareness. This is not a bad thing; it is a business model for how most NGOs operate. In building partnerships it is useful to disabuse ourselves of the notion that NGOs are inherently good and instead to focus on what each side can gain from collaboration.

I remember fondly a conversation I overheard in the atrium of London's Cottons Centre. I was waiting for a meeting nearby, having a sandwich, when I overheard a conversation between two colleagues. They were talking about how it is important to 'understand the competition' which can be done by 'signing up to their mail-lists, understand how they are going after clients and keep ahead of them by copying their tactics'. The senior woman was then coaching her junior in strategies to 'stay ahead of the competition' emphasising the importance of innovating to get the most 'sales'. This would all seem very normal. Except that both of the conversationalists worked for a major NGO.

We are not accustomed to thinking of NGOs in these terms. I do not seek to deride the important work that NGOs do, or to discredit them as useful partners, but it is important to understand that NGOs have a business model and that this creates some real risks – and opportunities – for collaboration.

Too many companies have worked with NGOs in good faith, opening up their operations in an attempt to improve their social and environmental performance, only to find themselves as the arch-villain in the NGO's next publicity campaign. In a way the long-term interests of NGOs, seen from a funding perspective, are inimical to actually *solving the problems* that they identify. Of course, some of these problems, such as childhood malnutrition, are of such an importance and scale that no moral hazard exists. But, for specific issues, such as worker rights, there are individuals and NGOs that have built their careers on the back of the problem. Some, but not all, seem more focused on perpetuating the story rather than arriving at a shared solution. Advocacy NGOs run this risk, because their very existence relies on having a serious and definable problem on which to focus.

Business–NGO collaboration can help to remove this moral hazard, providing long-term funding to help solve problems that are in the shared interests of business and society. This is the real opportunity of strategic CSR and NGO collaboration. It brings together the expertise, skills (and funding) of the private sector with the passion, the grass-roots connections and the capacities of the NGO sector. By altering the business model of NGOs towards one that rewards solving problems, companies can make a considerable contribution to society and to the voluntary sector. Companies then benefit by having competent, low-cost partners to implement CSR strategies. But successful collaboration needs to be built on a shared vision of how to achieve common goals. This requires *responsible* NGO partners and an understanding of the relative strengths and weaknesses of NGOs as partners.

Strengths and weaknesses

Understanding how NGOs work helps us to appreciate some of the relative strengths and weaknesses of the sector. Because the type and quality of NGOs varies greatly, we must be careful when making generalisations. But there are some general characteristics of the NGO sector that we should bear in mind. These relative strengths and weaknesses are different, perhaps complementary, to the strengths and weaknesses of the business community. It is in matching these skills that the opportunities for collaboration appear.

The strengths usually associated with NGOs, their core competences, are in having:

- Solid connections at the 'grass-roots' level, including local knowledge and an established presence

- Considerable experience working in poor/disadvantaged communities

- Legitimacy and public trust (brand value)

- A strong focus on public participation and the *process* of development

- A focus on a wide variety of issues

- Low cost structure

But for all the strengths of the NGO community, we also need to recognise that most NGOs have a set of weaknesses, which are somewhat inherent in their business model:

- A focus on problem identification without a wider perspective of the economic and political context of these problems

- Limited financial, managerial and organisational capacity

- Limited coordination with other NGOs and the wider development community

- Reliance on constant donations (the business model) and project-based funding, leading to a short-term problem focus rather than a solution focus

- Unaccountable work practices, based on an inherent assumption that the work they conduct is 'good' because the cause or problem is worthy

Looking at these generalised accounts of NGO strengths and weaknesses, we realise that in many ways they match. The ability of NGOs to work at the grass-roots level and their focus on problems among poor communities is directly related to the inability of NGOs to consider the wider economic context of these problems. They are too absorbed in the immediate issue to look at a wider perspective. Likewise, the low cost structure of many NGOs, with a reliance on volunteer time and placing most operations in the field, means that they are sometimes lacking in managerial and organisational skills. I have had exasperated clients talk to me about how 'unprofessional' their NGO partners are. This is not saying that NGO managers are bad at their jobs, rather that they lack the backup and support, the systems, that large companies have.

These strengths of being able to work at the 'grass-roots' level and the public trust in the NGO brand are areas not usually associated with businesses. NGOs are excellent at working in local communities, their local contacts are often hard to beat and in many cases NGOs have existing operations in places where large companies are simply not present. This sort of local-level work is exactly the area where companies do not normally have their strengths. NGOs, with their lower cost structure and existing infrastructure, have a comparative advantage in working at a community level. Whether your company is trying to target the 'fortune at the bottom of the pyramid' or to implement a dedicated CSR agenda in a poor community, the local contacts and infrastructure, matched with the low cost structure of NGOs, mean that they can be useful partners. NGOs also bring legitimacy, which is crucial to a successful CSR strategy.

Growing public mistrust of the corporate world, to which CSR is in part a response, means that companies and especially large corporations are mistrusted in many communities. Witness the negative effects for Coca-Cola of allegations of pesticide contamination of their products in India – a country long suspicious of Coca-Cola and other large brands. Any allegation made against companies by NGOs tends to gain media attention, while the denials, clarifications or corrections by companies are often dismissed as 'corporate bullshit'. Most people are much more willing to trust and work with NGOs than they are to work with companies. Given the NGO business cycle of fundraising based on publicity and the 'name and shame' game, the legitimacy accorded to NGOs is a core strength of the sector which itself poses a business risk. In the next section the strategies for tapping this potential and managing this risk are discussed.

However, the unquestioned legitimacy of NGOs is being eroded. Just as companies were once well trusted on the whole, until a number of transgressors gave 'big business' a bad name, so too has the NGO sector been let down by poor practices by some of its members. As the 'problems' identified by NGOs become more difficult to classify, with a business model that favours the creation of new problems, these problems become more controversial. While no one would dispute the worthiness of sating the victims of famine and curing disease, many other issues are somewhat more complex.

Take, for example, a recent article in the *International Herald Tribune*, discussing conservation efforts in the Brazilian rainforest:

> Depending on one's point of view, the World Wildlife Fund's financial support of a nature reserve here on the Rio Negro is either part of a laudable attempt to conserve the Amazon jungle – or the leading edge of a nefarious plot by foreign environmental groups to wrest control of the world's largest rain forest from Brazil and replace it with international rule (Rohter 2007).

One might have thought that wildlife preservation in Brazil would be universally agreed to be a good thing. It is easy to imagine any international company working in Brazil funding WWF's efforts at conservation as part of its CSR agenda. This

Box 6 **Pitfalls of partnership: a cautionary tale**

There are certainly risks to both sides in pursuing a partnership with an NGO. Witness for instance the internal split within Friends of the Earth (FoE) over the question of partnering with BSkyB, a UK broadcaster. Almost 100 staff (including most senior campaigners) signed a highly critical petition to the board opposing the alliance (Carrell 2007). Notably those FoE staff opposed to the move cited reputational risk as the main argument against the alliance, noting that a 'direct link to Sky would be highly divisive, damaging the group's reputation for not taking money from corporate interests and for campaigning against multinationals' (Carrell 2007).

Interestingly, competing environmental NGOs took this disagreement as an opportunity to cement their position as opposed to all forms of business collaboration. A spokesman for Greenpeace commented: 'We've an absolutely cast-iron position that we don't take any money from corporations. We're entirely funded by our members, so we wouldn't do that' (Carrell 2007).

This entrenched position against corporate partnerships is clearly unhelpful. But the public manner in which FoE staff aired their complaints also risked BSkyB's reputation, emphasising the importance of being careful when selecting potential partners. This is not to warn companies away from entering into partnerships, but it does reinforce the importance of conducting the same due diligence and risk management that you would for any other business partnership.

sort of charitable giving is considered part of the 'licence to operate' in such countries and conservation normally goes down well with shareholders. Herein lies a big risk for companies in working with NGOs. It would be very easy, to take the Brazilian example, for a foreign company through its charitable giving to be implicated (by some at least) in the 'nefarious plot . . . to wrest control of the world's largest rain forest from Brazil and replace it with international rule'. This would only play into traditional distrust of foreign companies and would weaken the company's brand. The lesson is theoretical in this case, but it still holds: your company's charitable giving and work with NGOs will reflect back on your company. This is why a strategic approach to NGO collaboration is so important.

Strategies for success

Having an understanding of what NGOs are, how their business model works and their strengths and weaknesses is an essential background to NGO collaboration. But this knowledge alone is not enough. What is needed is a strategy to make sure that the NGO partnership you choose makes sense, that both sides gain from it and that long-term issues — and risks — are managed as well as possible.

There is no single strategy for CSR, each different company has different needs and capacities and your CSR strategy should reflect this. Your company's CSR strategy should be part of its corporate strategy, building on its core competences and skills and using these in a way that further develops the business. So there are no magic solutions or quick fixes. Charitable giving, even to worthy causes, will not solve your CSR problems, because it does not directly address the specific responsibilities of your company's operations. It also means that you can't take advantage of the opportunities of CSR. To develop a CSR strategy for NGO engagement it is useful to go through a set of steps: to categorise your corporate responsibilities, to identify corporate opportunities, to recognise the areas where you need to partner and from this to manage the partnership in a manner that ensures accountability, the creation of shared value and risk sharing.

Categorise your corporate responsibilities and opportunities

Categorising your corporate responsibilities according to your operations was dealt with in Chapter 2. For areas of responsibility that are outside your core competence as an organisation, partnerships with NGOs can be one way of meeting these responsibilities. The crucial point to stress here is that identifying your company's responsibilities should be an internal process. While you should remain open to approaches from outside your organisation by keeping lines of communication with stakeholders open, relying on NGOs to identify your company's responsibilities is perilous. Because the NGO business model is built on identifying new issues, there is a risk that the NGO will focus on the newest or most fashionable issue, without substantively addressing the specific responsibilities of your company.

Once you have identified the specific and general issues of concern to your company, including the concerns of staff, shareholders and other stakeholders, then NGOs can be invited to share their ideas. Gildan, the company discussed in Chapter 4, has identified 'education' and 'youth' as two general issues for its operations in Canada. NGOs are invited to 'pitch' their idea for funding to a panel of staff, who then decide how to allocate funding. This process of encouraging staff participation then flows into a greater feeling of ownership as well as in ensuring that charitable giving is as effective as possible.

In looking at your responsibilities, it is also important to look for ways to turn your responsibilities into opportunities. How can your current challenges and threats be met in a way that enhances, rather than reduces, business performance? By looking at the long-term threats to your business operations you can begin to understand the areas in which your core competences can be used to effect a change in business climate. From this you can identify the opportunities for CSR within your industry. Again this is a process that needs to be conducted internally. While external input might be useful, drawing on NGOs at this stage is premature. It is more important to have an internal understanding and consensus on the specific responsibilities and opportunities for your company, and then build a strategy based on this. For problems where your own core competences don't exist and can't be developed, it becomes necessary to develop partnerships.

Recognise win–win opportunities

In looking to develop NGO cooperation for CSR, the default position is normally to turn to a large, well-established NGO. This is especially the case if companies are taking a *responsive* approach to CSR, reacting to previous problems and trying to 'fix' the problem as quickly as possible. This might be the solution for some problems, but it is not necessarily the right solution, nor is it a strategic solution for the long term. To build your strategy you need to identify the opportunities for partnership and seek out the right partners to meet your needs.

These steps are explained in Table 4 using the Turner Broadcasting Europe case study later in this chapter. However, we need to recognise that different industries have different partnership needs, for which a universal solution is not possible.

What we see in Table 4 is that, for most of the issues identified as corporate responsibilities for Turner, an internal opportunity exists. This is where the core competences of Turner can be leveraged to help address these responsibilities. But, for the wider responsibility, of helping to ameliorate some of the human suffering involved in the stories that Turner covers, a partnership is essential. Here, an international NGO, UNICEF, can lend both local implementation expertise and global legitimacy.

The point is that Turner identified this partnership opportunity as an area in which the company could benefit from engaging with NGOs. With this clear definition of where the opportunity existed, it is then important to define the value — to both parties — in this cooperation.

	Corporate responsibilities	Corporate opportunities	Partnership opportunities
	Issues where the company, through its operations, has a direct impact – positive or negative	*Issues on which the company has an influence where the company's core competences can be leveraged*	*Issues of key concern to the company where the company lacks the internal capacity to manage the issue*
Turner Broadcasting	◦ Accurate awareness raising and education ◦ Fair reporting on issues and promoting civil dialogue ◦ In Africa, to confront some of the human impacts of the stories that are covered by CNN and Turner	◦ Use Turner network to inform and educate the public ◦ Encourage documentaries and debates as well as news coverage ◦ Recognise that the internal capacity does not exist – so build a partnership to confront this responsibility	◦ No need to partner: capacity exists internally ◦ Collaboration is possible but not essential – internal capacity exists ◦ Forming a partnership with the Pepo project and UNICEF. Turner contributes finance and expertise, while UNICEF adds local capacity, legitimacy and implementation skills

Table 4 **Recognising win–win opportunities**

Creating shared value

For a partnership to work in the long run, both sides need to win. This is the sort of 'Chinese contract' explained in Chapter 3, of creating shared value on the basis of common values. Specific to the challenge of NGO collaboration for CSR is a need to define the limits and scope of the partnership, to identify the non-financial contributions that are required and to understand how the collaboration is perceived by both parties.

Cooperating with an NGO, or any business partner, is about finding external skills, resources and expertise that do not exist within your company. You need to be clear with potential partner organisations about the limits and scope of this collaboration. Which areas are you agreeing to work on? Which are you not? How free should the NGO feel to comment on the partnership? Will you only make joint statements, or are you both free to manage your own communications? In many ways the external perception will not follow these limits. Any partnership agreement between organisations tends to be perceived as a holistic agreement, which is why it is essential that you *know* and *trust* your partners, as described in detail in Chapter 3.

For the cooperation to work and to create shared value there needs to be more than a one-way donation of money. While finance is often part of agreements between business and NGOs, it is crucial — for both parties — that non-financial contributions are also made. When companies contribute their expertise, skills and resources to problems, better solutions can be arrived at. This ensures that the money is well spent and that the partnership actually builds something in the long term for the company, as well as helping to build capacity within the NGO. This is a two-way endeavour: company staff can learn from the NGO, building corporate competences in areas that are lacking. But for this to work there needs to be a common understanding of the purpose of the partnership.

A lack of a common understanding of why the partnership exists, and what each side hopes to gain, is a cause of many failed NGO–corporate collaborations. If the NGO is expecting donations without any sort of reciprocal agreement, then it is doubtful what your company will gain. Likewise, your company needs to be realistic about how much it can get from an NGO partner; a lack of capacity, as well as a need to retain some critical independence, may leave you feeling disappointed or betrayed. NGOs and businesses work in different worlds; they have different ways of operating and different expectations. Arriving at a shared understanding of what each side hopes to gain is central to creating shared value in the long run. Achieving this requires an element of risk sharing and accountability.

Risk sharing and accountability

As with any partnership, there is a need for joint contributions and for risk sharing. Again this is where you need to move beyond one-way donations of money, towards more meaningful NGO partnerships that are based on common contributions and shared risks. The biggest risk, to both sides, in corporate–NGO partnerships, is reputation risk.

An NGO's reputation, its brand, is one of its key advantages over other NGOs. For organisations such as the Red Cross — whose independence is central to its ability to do its job — reputation is sacrosanct. This means that some NGOs, for example Transparency International, refuse donations from governments on the basis that it might compromise their reputation for independence. This high moral stand is to be applauded. But, for most NGOs, this level of independence is not essential to their operations. On the contrary, greater connections and awareness of the wider economic development context could help NGOs do some of their work. This is where synergies exist: opportunities for companies and NGOs to work together to achieve shared goals.

Just as you seek to match corporate expertise, skills and money with NGOs who could benefit from these contributions, so too can NGOs contribute the expertise and contacts that your business lacks. In this sort of partnership, both sides are taking an operational and reputational risk. To manage this risk there need to be clear procedures in place, before things go wrong, which explain the limits of each party's responsibility. This risk management need not be any different from the procedures your company puts in place for any other business partnership, so long as both sides recognise that the relationship is more than a one-way donation of money — that it is a shared endeavour, with some shared risks, but one from which both sides seek to benefit.

Understanding exactly how each side benefits requires a level of accountability, not always evident in the NGO sector. Because NGOs work on worthy causes, operating at a 'grass-roots' level which is not easily monitored, they have tended to be free from questions about the real impact of their operations or the real motivations for their advocacy work. There has tended to be an assumption that NGOs' work is inherently 'good' and that they are to be trusted. This is starting to change.

The irresponsible use of power and funding by some NGOs has led to calls for greater accountability within the sector. Cases of NGO misconduct in advocacy, fundraising, management and oversight have led to greater caution among private donors and governments. This is a problem for the NGO sector to address internally, as it is beginning to do through initiatives such the UK NGO Accountability Forum administered by One World Trust.[72] The important point to note here is that due diligence is as important, if not more so, when entering into NGO partnerships as with any other business partnership.

Even where misconduct is not an issue, many of the large NGOs are already sufficiently well funded that they do not make the most deserving — or useful — partners. As one client commented to me, explaining an underperforming NGO partnership: 'they [the NGO] have too much money, they don't need our donation . . . which makes them lazy'.

In this case, there is no match between the financial needs of the NGO and the CSR strategy of the company, although there is a real need in the NGO for the company's expertise and skills. This illustrates the importance of having an open and accountable partnership as part of your CSR strategy.

The case study of Turner Broadcasting and UNICEF is in many ways a model example of how a company can leverage its core competences, combining these with an NGO in a strategic partnership, to create value for society, the company and the NGO. Turner has applied (and in some cases learned the hard way) the lessons from this chapter to produce a constructive NGO cooperation.

Case study: Turner Broadcasting Europe

Turner Broadcasting Europe, a division of Time Warner, has its core competences in communication. Through its main TV channels, CNN, Cartoon Network, TCM and other brands,[73] Turner communicates news, views and entertainment to millions throughout Europe, Africa and the Middle East on a daily basis. Often this includes reporting on natural disasters, conflicts, the impact of HIV/AIDS and other human tragedies. Turner is aware of its social responsibilities as a global news and entertainment provider, and its founder Ted Turner was an early leader in philanthropic giving. With few physical 'operations' it is necessary for Turner to use its core competence in communication to contribute to society and enhance its social mandate, beyond charitable giving. By providing free airtime, the use of cartoon characters and celebrities, publicity, design and communication expertise, Turner is able to contribute its core competence of communication to an effective NGO partnership with UNICEF. While Turner (and Time Warner) engages in considerable philanthropic giving, the most interesting aspect is how this money is backed up with expertise, airtime, publicity, staff participation and corporate support.

The key aspects of the Turner approach to CSR are: a focus on staff participation and volunteering, corporate input through airtime and engagement in issues that relate to the company's position as a news and entertainment provider. Although Turner has a number of different projects around the world, I identify here one example of a successful collaboration with UNICEF where Turner contributed its communication skills to good effect — creating shared value for the company, staff, society and its NGO partner. This has required key skills in managing partnerships (discussed in Chapter 3), which has not always been easy. But to ensure success in each of these collaborations Turner has been strategic in using its core competences for social responsibility in partnership with UNICEF.

Staff participation

Engaging staff in the CSR agenda of the company is central to Turner's CSR strategy. This occurs by encouraging volunteering, by promoting participation from staff at all levels in company CSR and by aligning corporate giving with staff interests. This ensures that the company's contribution is most useful to both corporate aims and to charitable recipients (NGO partners and wider society). With staff contributing their own core competences there is a sense of 'ownership' of the CSR strategy. This in turn helps with staff retention, in promoting diversity in the workplace and ultimately in promoting the company's core competences and corporate strategy.

Staff volunteering is encouraged for all Turner employees, who have 16 hours of paid volunteering time a year. There is a real emphasis on 'trying to match *skills* with *need*',[74] which ensures that staff gain the most out of their volunteering and that recipient organisations also benefit from special skills and competences. 'It is about making the best use we can of our assets' (Nick Hart, Head of CSR, Turner)

Volunteering at Turner is about more than providing labour and money; rather it is about using the skills that the company has and contributing them to the social good. This includes supporting cartoonists from Cartoon Network to help repaint a local school by drawing 'paint by numbers' cartoons on the walls. Successful volunteer programmes, such as assistance to London's homeless, have involved extended staff volunteer time, which the company supports as part of the CSR strategy. This support has been recognised by the Business in the Community PerCent Club, identifying Turner as among the UK's most generous companies, with nearly a quarter (24.2%) of staff involved in community activities. Staff are free to decide their own focus for volunteering and are encouraged, with the assistance of the CSR department, to find ways to involve the company.

For instance, Christiane Amanpour, Chief International Correspondent for CNN, made a documentary film, *Where Have All the Parents Gone?* which detailed the impact of HIV/AIDS on orphans in Kenya. This documentary spurred the company to engage with UNICEF in the Pepo Project (discussed below), including a visit by the company president to Kenya. To encourage staff involvement in this project, an essay competition was held with a prize of a visit to the project for two staff, which has proved to be an effective way to engage employees:

> By winning the trip and visiting the project, I am now really interested; I won't let it go . . . I have spent so much volunteer time on it now, but my boss has not complained once; they are really keen for me to be involved – I am probably a much more loyal employee now.[75]

The final comment, *I am probably a much more loyal employee now*, is where the corporate contribution starts to make business sense. By promoting volunteering and staff engagement, Turner is not only maximising its positive social contribution, it is *also* improving its corporate performance. Turner Europe's parent company, Turner Broadcasting System Inc., introduced volunteering as part of a broad philanthropic and CSR agenda. The concept has now been implemented in Turner Europe because of the positive impact it has on staff retention and performance. Going forward, Turner Europe sees staff volunteering as a good way to promote its 'Diversity Action Plan' to encourage greater diversity in the workplace. CSR successes, such as receiving coverage in *The Voice* (a London-based Afro-Caribbean paper), help to encourage diversity, especially from under-represented communities, which assists Turner in realising its goal of having a workforce as diverse as its audience.[76] 'It engages the company and our people with communities; as a communication company we need to engage with our audience' (Nick Hart, Head of CSR, Turner).

As a communication company, Turner's core competences are in its staff and their ability to engage with the audience. By involving staff in the CSR strategy of the company and by encouraging multiple approaches to reach diverse audiences, Turner promotes both public good and corporate strategy.

Communication as a CSR contribution

As a communication company, Turner has few 'operations' in the way that a manufacturing firm or energy company has. Thus there might seem to be fewer opportunities for CSR. This is a challenge that traditional CSR would have struggled to solve. Instead, Nick Hart, Head of CSR, points out that Turner has core competences in communication which are often lacking in the NGO and volunteer sectors. By pairing the skills of Turner's staff and the audience reach of their diverse channels, Turner has the opportunity to make a significant social contribution: one that provides key skills and resources to partners and that builds Turner's reputation and corporate performance.

In 2006 Turner contributed over £8 million worth of airtime and publicity to its CSR partners. This airtime allows charities to use Turner's resources to reach millions of viewers, sharing information and providing opportunities for giving: for instance, the annual 'Day for Change' public service announcement from UNICEF, which is aired on Cartoon Network. This is part of the 'Caretoon Network' initiative which aims to make younger audiences aware of the social and environmental problems around the world. This sort of awareness campaign is in line with Turner's role as a communication company, while also making a strong social contribution. Different audiences are educated using the different Turner channels: for example, a series of interviews with UNICEF's celebrity ambassadors presented on Turner Classic Movies. This airtime contribution, matched with Turner staff time and expertise, helps charities reach a much wider audience than they could otherwise. The benefits are significant: one viewer even sent in US$100,000 to UNICEF because of the publicity on CNN relating to the Pepo project.

Turner's contribution goes beyond free airtime. In recent years volunteer staff have created advertisements for the 'Theatre for a Change' charity, which were aired on CNN. Other volunteers have used their graphic design skills to create a logo for the Zamcog charity and designed charity gift cards. One of the staff involved in the visit to Kenya in 2006, Birgitte Johannsen, has used her multimedia design skills to design a website for the Pepo project[77] as part of an ongoing engagement in the project. At a corporate level, cartoon characters such as Scooby-Doo are frequently sent, along with gifts and donations, to charity functions and launches. Turner also gives permission for its well-known characters to front fundraising campaigns which are a great help to the charities while promoting the characters and demonstrating Turner's commitment to the community. These are all just a few examples of how communication, Turner's core competence, can be directed as part of the CSR strategy of the company.

By focusing on its core competences, Turner is better able to leverage its CSR spending to achieve the maximum benefit for recipients and to further develop Turner's own brand and core competences. But this CSR spending still needs to be directed and focused on areas that are relevant to the company.

Focus on relevant issues

The range of groups and projects with which Turner staff engage is incredibly broad. The company's CSR strategy involves work with everything from London-based charities to tsunami assistance and the Pepo project. Managing this diversity of interests and issues is a challenge for Turner, but this breadth of projects is central to Turner's aim of being as diverse as its audience. Still, it is necessary for Turner to focus on issues that are relevant to its staff, audience and shareholders. Equally important, these issues need to be ones where Turner's core competences can be leveraged effectively.

This is where the exercise of identifying your corporate responsibilities and opportunities is useful. In Table 1 (page 32) the hierarchy of social and environmental issues for a number of companies were identified. For Turner, a communication company reporting around the world, there are some general issues and responsibilities. By focusing on relevant issues where Turner's core competence in communication can be used, some corporate opportunities exist to further develop the brands and enhance the business strategy, as set out in Table 5.

Identifying the responsibilities of each different company is not an easy task, which is where staff involvement is a key. It identifies opportunities that management might otherwise be unaware of, it creates a sense of ownership within the company and it ensures the core competences are leveraged to their full effect. Crucial to ensuring that this contributes to company performance — that it is an investment and not an expense — is ensuring that the company focuses on relevant issues. A good example of this approach to issue identification — and opportunity creation — is the ongoing partnership between Turner Europe and UNICEF.

	General issues	Responsibilities	Opportunities
	Issues that concern society but which the company has little effect on and which do not materially affect its ability to do business	*Issues where the company, through its operations, has a direct impact – positive or negative*	*Issues which the company has focused on – and taken action – in a way that leverages core competences*
Turner Europe (CNN, Cartoon Network, Turner Classic Movies, etc.)	• HIV/AIDS • Conflict and civil wars • Income inequality	• Accurate awareness raising and education • Fair reporting on issues and promoting civil dialogue • In head office: promote diversity and opportunities. In operations: report on issues and build public awareness • In Africa: accurate reporting of poverty and other issues	• Use Turner network to inform and educate the public • Encourage documentaries and debates as well as news coverage • In London office: involvement with *The Big Issue* and homeless groups (incl. work experience for homeless) • Promoting 'CNN Debates' to raise awareness and engage in projects, such as Pepo

Table 5 **Turner's corporate responsibilities and opportunities**

Pepo la Tumaini Jangwani

CNN's Chief International Correspondent, Christiane Amanpour, visited the 'Wind of Hope in the Desert' or Pepo project, as part of a documentary on AIDS orphans in Africa.[78] From this documentary, Turner's CSR department recognised an opportunity to expand its existing partnership with UNICEF, providing greater funding and expertise while focusing on an identifiable project that staff could relate to. The strength of the Turner contribution is that it recognises the core competences of Turner and leverages these communication skills for greater benefit, in partnership with UNICEF. While a financial contribution is at the core of the company's contribution, staff volunteer time, Christmas gift baskets

donated by London staff and specific expertise – such as the Christiane Amanpour documentary – ensure an even wider impact for both Turner and UNICEF.
'Sending expertise is much more useful than sending money . . . the documentary was worth more than any corporate donation . . . there are more stories to tell
and we need Turner's help to put those stories out.'[79]

The Pepo project is focused on providing education, food and care for
HIV/AIDS orphans – and those affected by HIV/AIDS – in a rural village, Isiolo, in
northern Kenya. Founded and run by a local woman, Khadija Rama, and supported by UNICEF and other organisations, Pepo is emblematic of the sorts of
locally driven solution that exist in Africa. But these local solutions require external support, which is where organisations such as UNICEF come in. With core
competences in the areas of education, health and child protection, UNICEF has
the expertise on the ground to identify problems and implement solutions. It
would be wrong for Turner to do as some other firms do and pretend that it has
core competences in this area. Attempting to implement development and relief
operations is a specialised area, where the risks of 'getting it wrong' are not limited to wasted CSR expenditure, but can seriously jeopardise the lives of at-risk
and marginal groups. This is why it is crucial that companies focus on their core
competences and use these, in partnership with other organisations (as discussed
in the next chapter).

Turner's initial contribution to Pepo was a cash donation made through
UNICEF Kenya. This allowed projects to be expanded, such as increasing the scale
of a food assistance project and improving facilities at the local school and
orphanage. Almost immediately, this cash donation was eclipsed by the donations raised from the publicity that the CNN documentary created. By putting the
issue of AIDS orphans on the world stage and in personalising the tragedy, and
solution, with Pepo – the level of public awareness and charitable giving was
raised to an unprecedented level. It is in using Turner's core competence of communication – while also meeting company aims of staff engagement and promoting diversity – that the biggest contribution can be made. This also fed back
into the company, in a way that:

> touched people inside the corporation . . . I and my colleagues go
> out and report on famines, on wars, on torture, on terrorism, on HIV
> and AIDS – we are telling these stories. But it is great to work inside
> a corporation that realises that we are telling human stories.[80]

As the Turner partnership has developed, contributions that cost relatively little to the company, but which have a large impact on Pepo, have included increasing amounts of free airtime[81] and involvement of staff expertise, such as in establishing a promotional website (www.helppepo.com). The learning process from
this has been two-way. For instance, one team member in the UNICEF Nairobi

office discusses how her work in communications has been assisted by being exposed to 'professional, committed experts' such as those from Turner who taught her 'a great deal, technically and professionally'.[82] The same is true in the United Kingdom office of UNICEF, where communication staff have been exposed to Turner's operations. While finance still remains a core aspect of the Turner contribution, this has to be backed up with staff engagement and a contribution of core competences. Interestingly, this sort of donation of expertise and technology is increasingly important for well-financed organisations such as UNICEF. UNICEF recognises 'the need for partners and expertise . . . that technology and know-how are the biggest benefits the private sector can provide us'.[83]

The future of the Turner partnership with UNICEF and Pepo is in furthering Turner's contributions of expertise, staff time and skills, while backing this up with core funding to enable the Pepo project to operate.

> Our corporation has some of the best brains, the best talent, the best technology . . . we should use this to do some good in the world, which is essential for the survival of the rich and privileged, as well as for the survival of the poor (Christiane Amanpour).

This approach will enable Turner to utilise — indeed build — its core competences while making the maximum possible social contribution. In managing this partnership, the lessons of the next chapter on creating shared value will be important. The lesson here is to focus on what you know — in this case communication — and contribute it to a cause that meets the social responsibilities of the company.

Addendum

In 2008 Turner Broadcasting Europe worked with Habitat for Humanity on a home-building project for orphans in KwaZulu Natal. Twenty staff, including the heads of HR and CSR, conducted fundraising and travelled to KwaZulu Natal — raising over £30,000. In 2009 the company will conduct a similar partnership with PLAN in Mali, on a school-building project — which will include a camera crew to help raise the profile of educational projects in Mali

Conclusion

The purpose of this chapter is to apply the lessons from this book — leveraging your core competences, collaborating based on common values, going from global to local and managing evolution — and applying these to working with NGOs. The Turner case study is a good example of how core competences — with a little creative thinking and a commitment to partnership — can be leveraged to create shared value. In many ways NGOs are the natural partners for business. The areas in which NGOs lack skills and expertise are often those where businesses have a great deal to contribute. Equally, NGOs work in areas and ways that businesses find difficult to replicate. Companies need help in implementing their CSR strategies and NGOs have unique skills to contribute to this implementation.

Where the Turner case study is instructive is where it went through several steps. First an issue was identified by a member of staff, Christiane Amanpour, who used the Pepo project to illustrate a valid news story. This was then taken up by the CSR team as an issue that was of concern to the company and where the organisation's key skills in communication could be of assistance. The CSR department then took the initiative in setting up a partnership with UNICEF and the Pepo project, initially contributing funding, expanding this contribution to include expertise, donated airtime and communication skills. Third, and critically, staff in the London office have been engaged in the project, which has helped the company to meet its goals of promoting diversity and developing staff talent. There has also been a benefit in improving staff retention and helping people identify Turner — as a large corporation — with a very specific project in rural Kenya.

By going through this process and by leveraging Turner's core competences, the partnership has benefited both Pepo/UNICEF and Turner Broadcasting. The key lesson is that the contribution from Turner was not limited to cash donation, but also included a contribution of skills, staff expertise and staff involvement. The challenge going forward is in managing this partnership in a way that continues to bring benefit to both organisations.

The message of this chapter is that opportunities for collaboration are strong, but that there needs to be a genuine partnership. One-way donations of money, if they are not accompanied by expertise and corporate input, no longer suffice for CSR contribution. Corporate–NGO collaborations need to be built on shared contributions from each party, with a clear strategy to create shared value for both parties. Equally, risks need to be shared between the partners, which is why ensuring accountability in the partnership and with partner organisations is important. Putting this into practice requires a long-term commitment and understanding — from both companies and NGOs — based on shared value creation.

Creating shared value: the next steps

The challenges we face as communities, as companies and as individuals are immense. Global poverty, regional inequalities, climate change and local pollution can no longer be ignored. Businesses can play a positive role in helping to solve these problems; in so doing they enhance their legitimacy as well as create new opportunities for profit. This book has detailed how it is possible for companies to move beyond seeing corporate social responsibility as a cost, towards identifying the opportunities of strategic CSR. This strategic approach is about investing in CSR, to create long-term profitability and strategic advantage, as shown in the case studies from diverse companies. Underlying this approach is a belief in the power of businesses to create value. This value creation can, as the case studies illustrate, go beyond increasing shareholder returns. Rather, by looking to create *shared value*, companies can contribute to the societies and environment in which they operate. In doing this, they are investing in sustainable profits for the future.

Moving towards a shared value approach involves businesses, governments and NGOs, who need to coalesce around *common values*. It requires that companies continue to take their social and environmental responsibilities seriously, identifying how their operations impact on society and finding strategies to enhance the public good as well as private profit. The cases in this book have demonstrated how we need to stop looking at public good and private profit as opposing goals; instead we should see them as mutually reinforcing. Public good is enhanced when private profit is responsibly pursued. Likewise, companies rely on healthy societies and functional political systems for business to be viable.

This is not about promoting charity. Instead CSR is in the strategic interest of companies, while also being in the interests of society and the environment. This sort of strategic self-interest, or 'proper selfishness' — combined with a desire to live in healthy societies and environments — is the motivation for companies to develop their CSR strategies. There are sometimes tensions between the short-term interests of companies and the pressures on them in increasingly competitive markets. This is where governments, NGOs and societies can play an enabling role — in delivering a change in business climate — altering the system in which companies operate to one that rewards sustainable investments.

In achieving this, the future challenge lies in placing CSR at the mainstream rather than the periphery of company policy and operations. CSR needs to be more than a part of the publicity budget; it is about changing the way we do business. But it does not require us to sacrifice profitability, standards of living or environmental standards. Rather, CSR is central to achieving the sort of job creation, sustainable development, increasing consumer choices and innovation that hold the solutions to the problems we face today. By recognising that companies are not development agencies, the pressure for charitable giving (an expense) should be reduced. But companies are and can increasingly become *agents of development*.

By contributing their skills, expertise and effort, companies can make investments in creating value for society, investments that pay dividends in the long term and that are much more powerful agents of change than cash donations.

This book has provided six key lessons for businesses in using CSR to create shared value:

1. Leverage your core competence, as illustrated by Anglo American's Zimele initiative, creating value for society and enhancing the company's licence to operate — thus gaining competitive advantage

2. Collaborate based on common values, in order to achieve what would be impossible alone, as with Montana Exploradora and the AMAC initiative for community-based environmental protection in Guatemala

3. Operate globally but impact locally, as demonstrated by Gildan's worker- and environmentally friendly textile production in Central America and the Caribbean

4. Constantly evolve and change every step along the value chain, as Scandic Hotels has done in reducing waste, encouraging staff development and in implementing a 97% recyclable hotel room for the hospitality industry

5. Work with — rather than against — good governments to build flexible regulations — which incentivise responsible business practices — as with the WEE Directive in Norway

6. Cooperate with responsible NGOs in a constructive way, as with Turner Broadcasting Europe's partnership with UNICEF and other NGOs — where the company's core competences can best be leveraged

In addition there is a need for governments to change the institutions and 'rules of the game' within which business operates. In doing this, governments can play an enabling role for business, as in the example of electrical and electronic waste policy in Norway. Likewise, it is time for NGOs to take their own responsibilities seriously, engaging with companies rather than seeking to vilify them — and when this occurs there are some real opportunities for collaboration between NGOs and the private sector — driven by complementary core competences and common values.

None of these examples or case studies is perfect. They are real-world examples of different companies and organisations engaging in difficult problems. Some of these problems are directly related to corporate activities; some of the problems reflect the need for a wider 'licence to operate'. But none of these problems is easily solved or has simple solutions. Sometimes these companies have engaged in reaction to previous mistakes and problems, whereas some companies have been more proactive. The important lesson going forward is that it is possible for companies to change, to decide on a CSR strategy and to pursue it in collaboration with shareholders, stakeholders and society. Implementing this will entail creating new collaborations with NGOs and communities, as well as working with governments.

If you have read this book and been convinced of the need to implement strategic CSR, you could be wondering where to start. I make no pretence that strategic CSR is easy. It is not and shouldn't be. Easy choices, such as giving small donations to worthy charities, are not the sorts of choice that enable good companies to become great. Nor are easy solutions possible for the challenging and interlocking problems that we face today. But the good news is that, by using your company's key skills, you can contribute to society *and* enhance corporate performance. Sometimes this will require partnerships, it will certainly involve localising your operations in a responsible manner and it will require you to innovate.

Putting this into practice is best done in a series of steps . . .

Next steps

If you have read this far into the book, you are clearly interested in implementing CSR and supporting a change in business climate. Be bold: seek out a CSR strategy that is better than the competition. Your CSR strategy should define you and your organisation; it should also reflect the issues that matter to you, your shareholders and your community. Making this happen in practice will require you to go through a set of four steps, outlined in Figure 15. You will notice that this is presented as a circular process, not a flow chart. This is intentional, signalling the importance of constantly updating and challenging the CSR strategy to address new issues and create new opportunities.

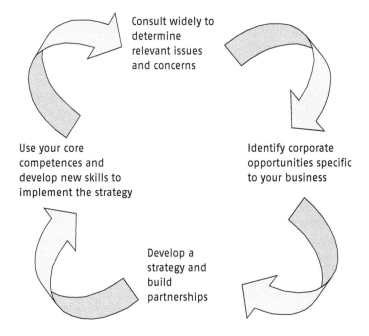

Consult widely to determine relevant issues and concerns

Identify corporate opportunities specific to your business

Use your core competences and develop new skills to implement the strategy

Develop a strategy and build partnerships

Figure 15 **Next steps**

Listen to your stakeholders

The first step is to begin to consult with others inside your business, organisation or government ministry. This stage is one of *listening to stakeholders*: shareholders, staff, suppliers and society about the issues that concern each different group. It is important that you are transparent about what your goals are — whether you are the CEO or a concerned employee — explain to others which issues matter to you and how these can fit within the corporate strategy. If you are clear where your search for value lies, and which corporate and personal values drive this, then you are in a much stronger position to create value — for your company and for wider society.

You need to begin by listing and prioritising the specific responsibilities for your company, including the social and environmental impacts (both positive and negative) that your operations are having. This can then be positioned within an analysis of the wider responsibilities of the organisation. Consultation with other organisations might also be useful, but remember that the responsibilities of your organisation are in concentric circles of responsibility, as shown in Figure 4 (page 19). In many cases you will already be aware of these issues and probably have ad hoc solutions in place. But it is necessary to go through this step to fully appreciate the importance that different stakeholders place on these issues; you may also discover new responsibilities and opportunities of which you were not previously aware. Beginning with this process, you need to start searching for partners who have value systems and goals in common with your organisation. There is little point in collaborating with partners who do not share your values and objectives, but with the right partners the opportunities for creating shared value are worthwhile.

Identify opportunities

The next step, and one where it might be useful to bring in external assistance and advice, is in identifying opportunities. This is where you identify that existing corporate responsibilities can be addressed in a way that creates cumulative advantage over your competition. These opportunities can come from being the 'first to market' with new initiatives, such as Tomra, or the benefits of taking a proactive stance on labour rights, as with Gildan. The point is that it is possible to turn *responsibilities* (a cost) into *opportunities* (an investment) in many cases. Sometimes meeting your corporate responsibilities is a necessary expense. But often advantage can still be gained by engaging staff and building your brand. CSR spending should be seen as an investment, in future profits and sustainability, an investment that produces value for shareholders as well as society.

Creative thinking is crucial to making a success of this step. Encouraging participation from staff, stakeholders and suppliers, as well as wider society, can help your company tap into ideas and new innovations. An external expert, coming in and asking the right questions, can be of assistance here. Although the solutions probably lie within your organisation, identifying these opportunities takes a degree of 'blue sky' thinking which can be hard for managers focused on day-today performance. But every bold business decision requires a degree of 'Knightian Uncertainty': a step into the unknown that is to some extent unmeasurable.[84]

The key to making sure that this uncertain step is certain to meet with success is in finding ways in which your core competences can be leveraged for CSR, which in turn should help develop the capacities of your organisation and prepare it to face new business challenges. By finding a way in which your core competences can be leveraged – through collaboration, taking operations from the global to the local and through constant evolution – you can begin to create shared value. Implementing this requires a clear strategy for utilising CSR in your business.

Develop a strategy

Developing a strategic approach to CSR is about aligning your corporate capacities with the corporate opportunities of CSR. It involves finding ways to leverage your core skills in a way that maximises the public good, while also developing these core competences and staff abilities. A well-worked-out CSR strategy will form part of overall corporate strategy. It will define how new markets are going to be entered, how new opportunities will be profited from and how the company will make the maximum possible returns to shareholders, staff, stakeholders and society.

In this way CSR and sustainability thinking needs to move from the periphery of your business, towards the core of corporate decision-making. This strategy might well include collaborating with NGOs and other organisations; it will certainly need a discussion of how other stakeholders are to be involved: the strategy must reflect company goals. Your CSR strategy should be seen as building on existing competences and corporate values, using these to create value for society and improve long-run profitability.

The strategy should set out an end ambition, explaining how the company's responsibilities are going to be reconciled into opportunities. In the long term, CSR strategy and corporate strategy should merge into the same planning and development process. By putting CSR strategy at the core of your decision-making process, you are correctly identifying the need to deliver value to shareholders, as well as society at large. This is a long-term investment, which can further enhance shareholder returns, if it is properly implemented.

Creating shared value through sustainability

Implementing a CSR strategy, moving from policy to practice, requires a great deal of management attention. Ensuring the success of any corporate strategy needs leadership and support from the top, combined with motivation and commitment throughout the organisation. CSR is no different. Partnerships need to be managed and partner organisations' expectations met. Staff need to be trained, upskilled and motivated to ensure the success of the strategy. A consistent, committed message from senior management is essential to managing this change. How you choose to implement your strategy should reflect the values of your organisation, it should demonstrate an understanding of the responsibilities specific to your company and it should illustrate an appreciation of the *opportunities* of CSR. This book has given a set of six guiding principles for *implementing CSR in difficult industries*:

- Leverage your core competences

- Collaborate based on common values

- Operate globally–impact locally

- Use evolution and revolution: to change at every step along the value chain

- Work with good governments to change the business climate

- Cooperate with responsible NGOs

These principles are grounded on an approach to *creating shared value* based on *common values.*

Creating shared value is not easy, but it is the best solution for the problems that we face today as businesses and as a society. If properly implemented, the shared value approach can deliver returns to businesses, society and the environment.

Acronyms and abbreviations

AMAC	Asociación de Monitoreo Ambiental Comunitario/Community Environmental Monitoring Committee (Guatemala)
BEE	Black Economic Empowerment
BOP	bottom of the pyramid
BTC	Baku–Tbilisi–Ceyhan pipeline
CBO	community-based organisation
CC	core competence
CEO	chief executive officer
CO_2	carbon dioxide
CSR	corporate social responsibility
EE	electrical and electronic (waste)
EITI	Extractive Industries Transparency Initiative
EPA	Environmental Protection Agency (USA)
EPR	extended producer responsibility
EU	European Union
FLA	Fair Labour Association
FMCG	fast-moving consumer goods
HLL	Hindustan Lever Limited
HR	human resources
IFC	International Finance Corporation
IPC	Instituto Politécnico Centroamericano/Central American Polytechnical Institute (Honduras)
IT	information technology
LSE	London stock exchange
MDG	Millennium Development Goal
MNC	multinational corporation
MSN	Maquila Solidarity Network
NGO	non-governmental organisation
PPP	public–private partnership
PR	public relations
R&D	research and development
RFID	radio frequency identification
SF6	sulphur hexafluoride
SFT	Norwegian Pollution Control Authority
TNS	The Natural Step
UNICEF	United Nations Children's Fund
USAID	US Agency for International Development
WCFCG	World Council for Corporate Governance
WEEE	Waste Electric and Electronic Equipment (EU Directive)
WFP	World Food Programme

Endnotes

Chapter 1

1   Different cultures see this in different ways. German industry, or 'Rhineland capitalism', has long considered employees as stakeholders. Buddhist economics, described in *Small is Beautiful* by E.F. Schumacher (1973), suggests that human development should be the goal of all economic activity. This has been taken up more recently by the King of Bhutan who stated that 'Gross National Happiness is more important than Gross National Product'. The United Nations Development Programme (UNDP) for Thailand likewise discusses the 'sufficiency economy' (www.undp.or.th/download/NHDR2007bookENG.pdf, accessed 8 July 2008). The important question in an increasingly globalised world is to arrive at common standards for CSR.

2   As an ethical question, there is a moral economy argument that privilege must be balanced by duty towards those who lack such privilege, obliging the privileged to take greater levels of responsibility. In international environmental law this is framed as a 'common but differentiated responsibility'.

3   The idea of legitimacy and the 'licence to operate' owes much to Rousseau's idea of a 'social contract' between rulers and citizens. The 'licence to operate' has been taken up in CSR thinking, for example, by BHP Billiton as part of its business case for CSR (sustainability.bhpbilliton.com/2005/repository/sustainabilityBHPBilliton/sustainable Development/businessCase.asp, accessed 8 July 2008).

4   www.hm-treasury.gov.uk/Independent_Reviews/stern_review_economics_climate_change, accessed 1 May 2008.

5   *Ibid.*

6   United Nations Development Programme, www.undp.kz/infobase/tables.html?id=192, accessed 1 May 2008.

7   www.economist.com/blogs/freeexchange/2006/12/income_inequality.cfm, accessed 1 May 2008.

8   See Chapter 10, 'Options for Action', in UNEP 2007.

9   For an excellent overview of these discussions, see May *et al.* 2007.

10 For a detailed academic study of corruption's impact on economic development, refer to Cooper-Drury *et al.* 2006.

11   IISD Commentary, www.iisd.org/pdf/2006/commentary_general_3.pdf, accessed 2 May 2008.

12   See Chapter 10, 'Options for Action', in UNEP 2007.

Chapter 2

13   This point is expounded clearly in Werther and Chandler 2006.

14   Title taken from *The Economist* 2005.

15   See 'Selling Health: Hindustan Lever Limited and the Soap Market' in Prahalad 2004.

16   The primary listing of the company was moved to the London Stock Exchange in 1999. For more corporate information, please consult www.angloamerican.co.uk, accessed 2 May 2008.

17   Personal communication with J. Samuel, 6 December 2007.

18   James Van Alstine, London School of Economics and Political Science, interviewed 26 November 2007.

19   Interview by author, 19 November 2007.

20   I am indebted to Jonathan Samuel at Anglo American for explaining the complex debate on the resource curse to me in more detail.

21   Interview by author, 29 January 2008.

22   Interview by author, 31 January 2008.

23   Interview with George Serobatse, 28 January 2008.

24   Interviewed by author, 16 November 2007.

25   Interview by author, 29 January 2008.

26   Interviewed by author, 16 November 2007.

27   Speech delivered 1 February 2008.

Chapter 3

28   Indian NGOs, www.ngosindia.com/ngos.php, accessed 8 July 2008.

29   For a much more detailed discussion of PPPs, refer to Link 2006.

30   PPPs have been especially prevalent in the construction and infrastructure sectors; see, for example, Cartlidge 2006.

31   www.unglobalcompact.org, accessed 6 May 2008.

32   Previously owned by Glamis Gold, now owned by Goldcorp and operated through its local subsidiary Montana Exploradora de Guatemala SA 'Montana'.

33   Interview by author, 22 November 2007.

34   Asociación de Monitoreo Ambiental Comunitario. Contact Bernarda Elizalde at elizalde@telus.net for more information.

35   Interview by author, 22 November 2007.

36   Interview by author, 12 December 2007.

Chapter 4

37   There are also some real risks associated with this strategy, as laid out in Wilson and Wilson 2006.

38 Interview by author, 27 November 2007.

39 For instance, the case of GAP in October 2007, where one garment from an entire fashion line (a girl's smock blouse) was alleged to have been made using child labour; yet considerable reputation and brand damage was endured by the company (news.bbc.co.uk/2/hi/south_asia/7066019.stm, accessed 6 May 2008).

40 www.localis-consulting.com, accessed 6 May 2008.

41 Interview with Laurence Sellyn, Executive Vice-President, Chief Financial and Administrative Officer, 22 May 2007.

42 Interview by author, 22 May 2007.

43 Instituto Politécnico Centroamericano, www.ipchn.org, accessed 6 May 2008.

44 Interview conducted by the author, 22 May 2007.

45 Isabel Rocha, Corporate Manager, Environment, 22 May 2007.

46 Corinne Adam, Director Corporate Social Responsibility, 22 May 2007.

47 *Ibid.*

48 Interview with Laurence Sellyn, 22 May 2007.

49 *Ibid.*

50 Interview by author, 10 July 2007.

51 Interview by author, 11 July 2007.

Chapter 5

52 See 'Selling Health: Hindustan Lever Limited and the Soap Market' in Prahalad 2004.

53 *Ibid.*

54 See www.britishairways.com/travel/csr-carbon-offsetting-trading/public/en_gb, accessed 8 July 2008.

55 Director of Corporate Social Responsibility and Safety & Security for Scandic. Interview by author. 21 March 2007.

56 Interview with J.P. Bergkvist conducted by the author on 21 March 2007.

57 *Ibid.*

58 Interview with David Cook, Chief Executive, The Natural Step International, conducted by the author , 30 March 2007.

59 www.tourismpartnership.org, accessed 8 May 2008.

Chapter 6

60 For more on the role of institutions and economic performance, see North 1990 and 1993.

61 The Ethical Investment Association, www.ethicalinvestment.org.uk, accessed 8 May 2008.

62 Including the Nordic countries of Sweden, Denmark, Norway, Finland and Iceland; www.svanen.nu/Eng, accessed 8 May 2008.

63 Interview with Radnar Unge, Managing Director, SIS Ecolabelling Sweden, conducted by the author, 20 March 2007.

64 www.theage.com.au/news/business/bca-fights-social-responsibility-law/2005/10/16/1129401144710.html, accessed 8 May 2008.

65 The *dombra* is a local musical instrument.
66 Interview with Kari Aa, SFT, conducted by the author, 23 March 2007.
67 Interview with Rune Opheim, SFT, conducted by the author, 23 March 2007.
68 El-retur Annual Report 2005, www.elretur.no/MiljorapportEN2005.pdf, accessed 8 May 2008.
69 Described in international innovation literature as the 'Porter hypothesis'.

Chapter 7

70 World Bank: Poverty and Social Impact Analysis Glossary, go.worldbank.org/7BKU4R5560, accessed 9 May 2008.
71 Amnesty International; www.amnesty.org/en/news-and-updates/feature-stories/blood-diamonds-are-still-reality-20070123, accessed 8 July 2008.
72 www.oneworldtrust.org/?display=project&pid=12, accessed 9 May 2008.
73 Turner Broadcasting Europe is responsible for channels including CNN, TCM (Turner Classic Movies), Cartoon Network, Cartoon Network Too, Cartoonito, Toonami and Boomerang.
74 Interview with Nick Hart, Head of CSR at Turner Broadcasting Europe, 14 May 2007.
75 Interview with Birgitte Johannsen, multimedia designer at Turner, conducted by the author, 14 May 2007.
76 In 2007 Time Warner (Turner's parent company) was ranked among the top 100 employers in the UK in Stonewall's Workplace Equality Index.
77 www.helppepo.com, accessed 9 May 2008.
78 *Where Have All The Parents Gone?* (CNN©).
79 Interview with Roger Pearson, Deputy Representative UNICEF Kenya, conducted by the author, 19 July 2007.
80 Interview with Christiane Amanpour conducted by the author, 1 August 2007.
81 Provided to the UNICEF National Committee of the United Kingdom.
82 Interview with Juliet Otieno conducted by the author, 19 July 2007.
83 Yasamura Kimura, UNICEF Regional Fundraising/Marketing Officer, Asia and Africa, interviewed on 17 July 2007.

Chapter 0

84 Named after Frank Knight and his 1921 book *Risk, Uncertainty and Profit*.

References

Auty, R.M. (1993) *Sustaining Development in Mineral Economies: The Resource Curse Thesis* (Abingdon, UK: Routledge).

Averill, V. (2007) 'African trade fears carbon footprint backlash', BBC News; news.bbc.co.uk/2/hi/business/6383687.stm, accessed 29 April 2008.

Blake, Dawson, Waldron Lawyers (2006) 'Company Law and Governance Update' (August 2006); available on request from marketing@bdw.com.

Carrell, S. (2007) 'Plan to link up with BSkyB splits Friends of the Earth', *The Guardian*, 6 August 2007.

Carrol, C. (2007) 'Reflections on Corporate Responsibility from the Extractive Sector', keynote address at the *Business for Social Responsibility 2007 Conference*, San Francisco, 23–26 October 2007.

Cartlidge, D. (2006) *Public Private Partnerships in Construction* (Abingdon, UK: Taylor & Francis).

Christmann, P., and G. Taylor (2001) 'Globalization and the Environment: Determinants of Firm Self-regulation in China', *Journal of International Business Studies* 32.3: 439-58.

Collier, P. (2007) *The Bottom Billion: Why the poorest countries are failing and what can be done about it* (New York: Oxford University Press).

Cooper-Drury, A., J. Krieckhaus and M. Lusztig (2006) 'Corruption, Democracy, and Economic Growth', *International Political Science Review* 27.2: 121-36.

Davis, I. (2005) 'The Biggest Contract', *The Economist*, 26 May 2005.

Dempsey, M. (2007) 'Malta woos technology wanderers', BBC News, 9 August 2007; news.bbc.co.uk/2/hi/business/6912215.stm, accessed 29 April 2008.

The Economist (2005) 'The Union of Concerned Executives', *The Economist*, 20 January 2005.

—— (2006) 'Good Food', *The Economist*, 7 December 2006.

—— (2007a) 'In Search of the Good Company', *The Economist*, 6 September 2007.

—— (2007b) 'Planes, Prizes and Perfect PR', *The Economist*, 13 February 2007.

Environmental Justice Foundation (2005) 'White Gold: The True Cost of Cotton – Uzbekistan, Cotton and the Crushing of a Nation'; www.ejfoundation.org/pdf/white_gold_the_true_cost_of_cotton.pdf, accessed 29 April 2008.

Findlay, R. (2007) 'Cross-sector Partnership as an Approach to Inclusive Development', paper presented at the UNRISD Conference, *Business, Social Policy and Corporate Political Influence in Developing Countries*, Geneva, Switzerland, 12–13 November 2007.

Friedman, M. (1962) *Capitalism and Freedom* (Chicago: University of Chicago Press).

Frohlich, M.T., and R. Westbrook (2001) 'Arcs of Integration: An International Study of Supply Chain Strategies', *Journal of Operations Management* 19: 185-200.

Hamel, G. (2000) *Leading the Revolution* (Boston, MA: Harvard Business School Press).

Handy, C.B. (1995) *The Empty Raincoat: Making Sense of the Future* (London: Random House Business Books).

—— (1997) *The Hungry Spirit: Beyond Capitalism – A Quest for Purpose in the Modern World* (London: Hutchinson).

Hawkins, D.E. (2006) *Corporate Social Responsibility: Balancing Tomorrow's Sustainability and Today's Profitability* (Basingstoke, UK: Palgrave Macmillan).

Hawksley, H. (2007) 'Child Cocoa Workers Still "Exploited" ', BBC News, Ivory Coast; news.bbc.co.uk/2/hi/africa/6517695.stm, accessed 29 April 2008.

Henriques, A., and J. Richardson (2004) *The Triple Bottom Line: Does It All Add Up? Assessing the Sustainability of Business and CSR* (London: Earthscan).

Hochschild, A. (2005) *Bury the Chains: Prophets and Rebels in the Fight to Free an Empire's Slaves* (Boston, MA: Houghton Mifflin).

IFC (International Finance Corporation) (2006) 'Lesson of Experience: The Baku–Tbilisi–Ceyhan (BTC) Pipeline Project'; www.ifc.org/ifcext/enviro.nsf/AttachmentsByTitle/p_BTC_LessonsLearned/$FILE/BTC_LOE_Final.pdf, accessed 29 April 2008.

—— (2007) 'Participatory Environmental Monitoring, Guatemala', CommDev; commdev.org/section/projects/participatory_environmental_mo, accessed 29 April 2008.

Jones, I.W., M. Pollitt and D. Bek (2007) *Multinationals in Their Communities: A Social Capital Approach to Corporate Citizenship Projects* (Basingstoke, UK: Palgrave Macmillan).

Kotler, P., and N. Lee (2005) *Corporate Social Responsibility: Doing the Most Good for Your Company and Your Cause* (New York: John Wiley).

Lee, C.Y., and K. Røine (2004) *Extended Producer Responsibility Stimulating Technological Changes and Innovation: Case Study in the Norwegian Electrical and Electronic Industry* (Report 1/2004, working papers of the Norwegian University of Science and Technology: Program for industriell økologi; Trondheim, Norway: Norwegian University of Science and Technology).

Liker, J. (2003) *The Toyota Way* (New York: McGraw-Hill).

Link, A.N. (2006) *Public/Private Partnerships: Innovation Strategies and Policy Alternatives* (New York: Springer-Verlag).

Lodge, G.C., and C. Wilson (2007) 'What a UN Partnership with Big Business Could Accomplish', *Harvard Business Review*, 21 February 2007.

May, S.K., G. Cheney and J. Roper (eds.) (2007) *The Debate over Corporate Social Responsibility* (Oxford, UK: Oxford University Press).

Murray, S. (2005) 'Good logistics offer better relief: partnerships between relief organisations and logistics companies bring a new approach to disaster management', *Financial Times*, 16 December 2005: 6.

Nattrass, B., and M. Altomare (2007) 'The Natural Step Organizational Case Summary: Scandic Hotels AB'; www.naturalstep.org.nz/downloads/International_Case_Study_pdfs/TNSI_Scandic_Hotels.pdf, accessed 29 April 2008.

North, D.C. (1990) *Institutions, Institutional Change, and Economic Performance* (Cambridge, UK: Cambridge University Press).

—— (1993) *New Institutional Economics and Development* (Working Paper; St Louis, MO: Washington University).

OECD (Organisation for Economic Cooperation and Development) (2007) 'Assessing Environmental Policies', OECD Policy Brief; www.oecd.org/dataoecd/52/15/38208236.pdf, accessed 29 April 2008.

Orlitzky, M., F.L. Schmidt and S.L. Rynes (2003) 'Corporate Social and Financial Performance: A Meta-analysis', *Organization Studies* 24.3: 403-41.

Porter, M.E., and M.R. Kramer (2006) 'Strategy and Society: The Link between Competitive Advantage and Corporate Social Responsibility', *Harvard Business Review* 84.12: 78-92.

Prahalad, C.K. (2004) *The Fortune at the Bottom of the Pyramid: Eradicating Poverty through Profits* (Upper Saddle River, NJ: Wharton School Publishing).

—— and G. Hamel (1990) 'The Core Competence of the Corporation', *Harvard Business Review*, May/June 1990: 79-91.

Pyndt, J., and T. Pedersen (2005) *Managing Global Offshoring Strategies: A Case Approach* (Copenhagen: Copenhagen Business School Press).

Reich, R. (2007) *Supercapitalism: The Transformation of Business, Democracy and Everyday Life* (New York: Borzoi Books).

Rohter, L. (2007) 'In the Amazon: Conservation or Colonialism?', *International Herald Tribune*, 26 July 2007; www.iht.com/articles/2007/07/27/america/27amazon-web.php, accessed 8 July 2008.

Rowe, J. (2005) 'Corporate Social Responsibility as Business Strategy', Center for Global, International and Regional Studies, University of California, Santa Cruz; repositories.cdlib.org/cgirs/reprint/CGIRS-Reprint-2005-08, accessed 29 April 2008.

Roy, A. (2004) 'Help That Hinders', *Le Monde Diplomatique*, November 2004.

Schumacher, E.F. (1973) *Small is Beautiful: Economics as if People Mattered* (London: HarperCollins).

Schumpeter, J. (1942) *Capitalism, Socialism and Democracy*.

Soros, G. (2000) *Open Society: Reforming Global Capitalism* (New York: Public Affairs).

Stiglitz, J. (2007) *Making Globalization Work: The Next Steps to Global Justice* (London: Penguin).

Stott, L. (2007) *Conflicting Cultures: Lessons from a UN–Business Partnership* (London: International Business Leaders Forum).

Taylor, R. (2006) 'The Greening of the Hotel Industry', *The Guardian*, 24 November 2006.

Tepper Marlin, A., and J. Tepper Marlin (2003) 'A Brief History of Social Reporting', *Business Respect* 51 (March 2003); www.mallenbaker.net/csr/CSRfiles/page.php?Story_ID=857, accessed 8 July 2008.

UN Millennium Project (2006) *Investing in Development: A Practical Plan to Achieve the Millennium Development Goals* (Report to the UN Secretary-General; London: Earthscan).

UNEP (United Nations Environment Programme) (2007) *Global Environment Outlook: Environment for Development* (Nairobi, Kenya: UNEP).

Vogel, D. (2006) *The Market for Virtue: The Potential and Limits of Corporate Social Responsibility* (Washington, DC: Brookings Institution).

Wall, C. (2007) 'Kazakh Public Policy and Corporate Social Responsibility: An Analysis of Health Care Provision in an Era of CSR and Kazakh Nationalism', paper presented at the *Conference on Business, Social Policy and Corporate Political Influence in Developing Countries*, UNRISD, Geneva, 12–13 November 2007.

Ward, H. (2005) 'Corporate Responsibility and the Business of Law', International Institute for Environment and Development; www.iied.org/SM/CR/documents/Corporateresponsibilityandthebusinessoflaw.pdf, accessed 29 April 2008.

WEF (World Economic Forum) (2005) *Building on the Monterrey Consensus: The Growing Role for Public–Private Partnerships in Mobilising Resources for Development* (Geneva: WEF): 23.

Weiser, J., M. Kahane, S. Rochlin and J. Landis (2006) *Untapped: Creating Value in Underserved Markets* (San Francisco: Berrett-Koehler).

Werther, W., and D. Chandler (2006) *Strategic Corporate Social Responsibility: Stakeholders in a Global Environment* (Thousand Oaks, CA: Sage Publications).

Wilson, C., and P. Wilson (2006) *Make Poverty Business: Increase Profits and Reduce Risks by Engaging with the Poor* (Sheffield, UK: Greenleaf Publishing).

Wolf, M. (2005) *Why Globalization Works* (New Haven, CT: Yale Nota Bene).

World Bank (2007) 'Overview: Understanding Poverty'; go.worldbank.org/RQBDCTUXW0, accessed 29 April 2008.

Index

NOTE: page numbers in *italic* figures refer to figures, tables and boxes in the text.

CCs
see Core competences
Central American Polytechnical Institute
see IPC
Challenges
social and environmental   12-18
Charity
charity-based localisation   75
cookie-cutter CSR   50, 90, 121
investing in long-term relationships   84
public perception of CSR   5, 9-10, 11
Turner contribution to Pepo project   152-3
see also Corporate philanthropy
Chile
Anglo American programme   45
China
increasing environmental standards   73
Choice
giving voice to choice   96-7
Circles of influence and responsibility   18, 19,
24, 115, 159
Citizenship
see Corporate citizenship
'Clean-up' cost for pollution
environmental pricing   119
Climate change
implications   14-15
requiring revolutionary change   100
response to   x, xi-xii, xiii
CO₂ emissions
buying carbon offsets   96, 120
Coca-Cola   140
Coffee market
fair trade   96, 98-9, 107
Collaboration   47-65
AMAC and Montana Exploradora   60-4
strategic opportunities   54-5
see also Partnerships; Strategic partnerships
'Collective' responsibility
preferred by industry   125
Commercial benefit
Norway's EE waste policy   128
Communication
CSR contribution   149-50
enabling resolution of issues   83-4
Community based organisations (CBOs)   134,
135
Community consultation
identifying needs and issues   76
Community development
changing business climate   73-5
Community empowerment
benefits of going local   66-7
Community engagement
Gildan case study   83, 86
Competences
see Core competences
Competitive advantage
Anglo Zimele   44-5, 46
creating   90
see also Sustained competitive advantage

Consent
local, relied on in mining industry   64
Consumers
benefits of going local   66-7
engaging with   96-7
Contractors
Gildan's long-term agreements   82
Contracts
partnerships and strategic CSR   53
short-term outsourcing   72
Core business approach
creating 'shared value'   36
Core competences (CCs)
Anglo American's contribution to Zimele   40-
1, 42-3, 45-6
complementing with CSR   30-5, 32, 34
extractive industry supporting local businesses
73
HLL's processing consumer products   93
identifying   29-30, 31
innovation by commitment to   89-90
Montana's contribution to AMAC   61, 64-5
of NGOs   139
Omtanke as Scandic's   103-4
required in localising operations   67
strategic partnership opportunities   47, 51
to enhance competitive advantage   91
Turner–UNICEF partnership   147-9
understanding and harnessing   24-5
UNICEF   152
Core weaknesses
of NGOs   139
Corporate citizenship   69-70
Corporate philanthropy   30, 32
Corporate reporting
'stakeholder' approach   8-9
Corporate social charity   9-10
Corporate social responsibility (CSR)
achieving social benefit   77
catalysing local economic development   73-5
continuum   17, 17
cookie-cutter CSR   50, 90, 121
CSR as corporate strategy   78-83
as good management   25-9
government role   111-12
history   7-12
implementation   2-4, 3
innovation on supply chain   97, 99
as investment   4-5, 6, 10
'living wage' initiative   71
going local: a win–win example   66-7
and NGO partnerships   131-54, 141
opportunity, not threat   1-2
partnerships to create shared value   47-65
policies and procedures   9-10
priorities visualised as circles   18, 19, 24, 115,
159
responsive CSR   32-3
Turner's corporate responsibilities   150, 151
see also Strategic CSR